My Revision Notes

OCR GCSE (9–1)
ECONOMICS

Jan Miles-Kingston
Clive Riches

HODDER
EDUCATION
AN HACHETTE UK COMPANY

Acknowledgements

Every effort has been made to trace all copyright holders, but if any have been inadvertently overlooked, the Publishers will be pleased to make the necessary arrangements at the first opportunity.

Although every effort has been made to ensure that website addresses are correct at time of going to press, Hodder Education cannot be held responsible for the content of any website mentioned in this book. It is sometimes possible to find a relocated web page by typing in the address of the home page for a website in the URL window of your browser.

Hachette UK's policy is to use papers that are natural, renewable and recyclable products and made from wood grown in well-managed forests and other controlled sources. The logging and manufacturing processes are expected to conform to the environmental regulations of the country of origin.

Orders: please contact Hachette UK Distribution, Hely Hutchinson Centre, Milton Road, Didcot, Oxfordshire, OX11 7HH. Telephone: (44) 01235 827827. Email education@hachette.co.uk Lines are open from 9 a.m. to 5 p.m., Monday to Friday. You can also order through our website: www.hoddereducation.co.uk

ISBN: 978 1 5104 7218 1

© Jan Miles-Kingston and Clive Riches 2020

First published in 2020 by

Hodder Education,

An Hachette UK Company

Carmelite House

50 Victoria Embankment

London EC4Y 0DZ

www.hoddereducation.co.uk

Impression number 10 9 8

Year   2024

All rights reserved. Apart from any use permitted under UK copyright law, no part of this publication may be reproduced or transmitted in any form or by any means, electronic or mechanical, including photocopying and recording, or held within any information storage and retrieval system, without permission in writing from the publisher or under licence from the Copyright Licensing Agency Limited. Further details of such licences (for reprographic reproduction) may be obtained from the Copyright Licensing Agency Limited, www.cla.co.uk

Cover photo: Sy Sarayut/Adobe

Typeset by Integra Software Services Pvt. Ltd., Pondicherry, India

Printed in India

A catalogue record for this title is available from the British Library.

Get the most from this book

Everyone has to decide his or her own revision strategy, but it is essential to review your work, learn it and test your understanding. These Revision Notes will help you to do that in a planned way, topic by topic. Use this book as the cornerstone of your revision and don't hesitate to write in it — personalise your notes and check your progress by ticking off each section as you revise.

Tick to track your progress

Use the revision planner on pages 4–8 to plan your revision, topic by topic. Tick each box when you have:
- revised and understood a topic
- tested yourself
- practised the exam and 'Now test yourself' questions and gone online to check your answers and complete the quick quizzes

You can also keep track of your revision by ticking off each topic heading in the book. You may find it helpful to add your own notes as you work through each topic.

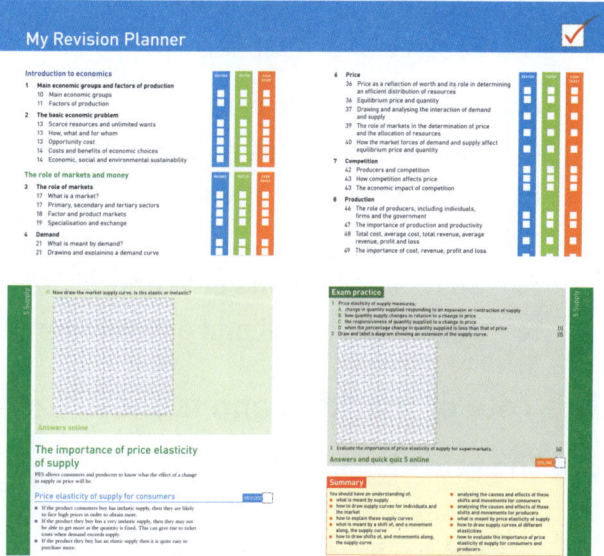

Features to help you succeed

Exam tips
Expert tips are given throughout the book to help you polish your exam technique in order to maximise your chances in the exam.

Typical mistakes
The author identifies the typical mistakes candidates make and explains how you can avoid them.

Now test yourself
These short, knowledge-based questions provide the first step in testing your learning. Answers are online.

Definitions and key words
Clear, concise definitions of essential key terms are provided where they first appear.

Key words from the specification are highlighted in purple throughout the book.

Revision activities
These activities will help you to understand each topic in an interactive way.

Debates
Debates are highlighted to help you assess arguments and use evidence appropriately.

Exam practice
Practice exam questions are provided for each topic. Use them to consolidate your revision and practise your exam skills.

Summaries
The summaries provide a quick-check bullet list for each topic.

Online
Go online to check your answers to the 'Now test yourself' and exam questions, and try out the extra quick quizzes at **www.hoddereducation.co.uk/myrevisionnotesdownloads**

OCR GCSE (9-1) Economics 3

My Revision Planner

Introduction to economics

1 Main economic groups and factors of production
- 10 Main economic groups
- 11 Factors of production

2 The basic economic problem
- 13 Scarce resources and unlimited wants
- 13 How, what and for whom
- 13 Opportunity cost
- 14 Costs and benefits of economic choices
- 14 Economic, social and environmental sustainability

The role of markets and money

3 The role of markets
- 17 What is a market?
- 17 Primary, secondary and tertiary sectors
- 18 Factor and product markets
- 19 Specialisation and exchange

4 Demand
- 21 What is meant by demand?
- 21 Drawing and explaining a demand curve
- 23 Drawing shifts of, and movements along, the demand curve
- 24 Causes and consequences of shifts of, and movements along, the demand curve
- 25 Price elasticity of demand
- 26 Drawing demand curves of different elasticity
- 27 The importance of price elasticity of demand

5 Supply
- 28 What is meant by supply?
- 28 Drawing and explaining a supply curve
- 30 Drawing shifts of, and movements along, the supply curve
- 31 Causes and consequences of shifts of, and movements along, the supply curve
- 32 Price elasticity of supply
- 33 Drawing supply curves of different elasticity
- 34 The importance of price elasticity of supply

Answers and quick quizzes at www.hoddereducation.co.uk/myrevisionnotesdownloads

6 Price
- 36 Price as a reflection of worth and its role in determining an efficient distribution of resources
- 36 Equilibrium price and quantity
- 37 Drawing and analysing the interaction of demand and supply
- 39 The role of markets in the determination of price and the allocation of resources
- 40 How the market forces of demand and supply affect equilibrium price and quantity

7 Competition
- 42 Producers and competition
- 43 How competition affects price
- 43 The economic impact of competition

8 Production
- 46 The role of producers, including individuals, firms and the government
- 47 The importance of production and productivity
- 48 Total cost, average cost, total revenue, average revenue, profit and loss
- 49 The importance of cost, revenue, profit and loss for producers
- 50 Economies of scale

9 The labour market
- 52 The role and operation of the labour market
- 53 The determination of wages through supply and demand
- 56 Gross and net pay

10 The role of money and financial markets
- 58 The role of money as a medium of exchange
- 58 The role of the financial sector
- 60 The importance of the financial sector
- 61 How different interest rates affect the levels of saving, borrowing and investment
- 62 The effect on savings and borrowings of changes in the rate of interest

OCR GCSE (9–1) Economics

Economic objectives and the role of government

11 Economic growth
- 64 Meaning of economic growth
- 64 Measurement of economic growth
- 65 Recent and historical data
- 66 Determinants of economic growth
- 68 Costs and benefits of economic growth
- 68 Economic, social and environmental sustainability

12 Low unemployment
- 70 Employment and unemployment
- 70 The Claimant Count
- 71 Calculation of unemployment rate
- 71 Recent and historical data
- 72 Causes and types of unemployment
- 73 Consequences of unemployment

13 Fair distribution of income
- 75 Meaning of distribution of income
- 75 Types of income
- 75 Difference between income and wealth
- 76 Calculation of income and wealth
- 76 Causes of differences in distribution of income and wealth
- 77 Consequences of differences in distribution of income and wealth

14 Price stability
- 79 Price stability and inflation
- 79 Real and nominal values
- 79 Measurement of inflation: consumer price index (CPI)
- 79 Calculation of the effect of inflation on prices
- 80 Recent and historical data
- 81 Causes of inflation
- 81 Consequences of inflation

15 Fiscal policy
- 84 The purposes of government spending and sources of government revenue
- 86 Government budgets
- 86 Fiscal policy/economic objectives
- 87 How taxes and spending affect markets and the economy
- 88 The costs and benefits of fiscal policy
- 89 Economic consequences of measures to redistribute income and wealth

Answers and quick quizzes at www.hoddereducation.co.uk/myrevisionnotesdownloads

16 Monetary policy
- 91 Monetary policy and how it can be used to achieve economic objectives
- 92 How monetary policy can affect growth, employment and price stability
- 93 The effects of monetary policy

17 Supply-side policy
- 96 Supply-side policy and economic objectives
- 97 The costs and benefits of supply-side policies

18 Limitations of markets
- 99 Externalities
- 100 Government policies to correct externalities
- 100 Taxation
- 100 Taxation to correct externalities
- 101 Subsidies
- 101 Subsidies to correct externalities
- 102 State provision
- 103 State provision to correct externalities
- 103 Legislation and regulation
- 104 Legislation and regulation to correct externalities
- 104 Information provision
- 105 Information provision to correct externalities

International trade and the global economy

19 Importance of international trade
- 106 Reasons for countries to trade
- 106 Benefits of imports and exports
- 107 Free trade agreements
- 107 The European Union (EU)

20 Balance of payments
- 109 Balance of payments on current account
- 110 Calculation of deficits and surpluses
- 111 Recent and historical data
- 111 The importance of the current account to the UK economy
- 112 Causes of surplus and deficit of the current account

21 Exchange rates
- 114 Drawing and analysing exchange rate diagrams
- 117 Calculation of currency conversion
- 117 Recent and historical data
- 118 The effect of changes in the exchange rate

REVISED   TESTED   EXAM READY

OCR GCSE (9–1) Economics

22 Globalisation
   120 The meaning of globalisation
   120 Driving factors of globalisation
   121 Measurement of development
   122 Costs and benefits of globalisation

Countdown to my exams

6–8 weeks to go

- Start by looking at the specification — make sure you know exactly what material you need to revise and the style of the examination. Use the revision planner on pages 4–8 to familiarise yourself with the topics.
- Organise your notes, making sure you have covered everything on the specification. The revision planner will help you to group your notes into topics.
- Work out a realistic revision plan that will allow you time for relaxation. Set aside days and times for all the subjects that you need to study, and stick to your timetable.
- Set yourself sensible targets. Break your revision down into focused sessions of around 40 minutes, divided by breaks. These Revision Notes organise the basic facts into short, memorable sections to make revising easier.

REVISED ☐

2–6 weeks to go

- Read through the relevant sections of this book and refer to the exam tips, exam summaries, typical mistakes and key terms. Tick off the topics as you feel confident about them. Highlight those topics you find difficult and look at them again in detail.
- Test your understanding of each topic by working through the 'Now test yourself' questions in the book. Look up the answers online.
- Make a note of any problem areas as you revise, and ask your teacher to go over these in class.
- Look at past papers. They are one of the best ways to revise and practise your exam skills. Write or prepare planned answers to the exam practice questions provided in this book. Check your answers online and try out the extra quick quizzes at www.hoddereducation.co.uk/myrevisionnotesdownloads
- Use the revision activities to try out different revision methods. For example, you can make notes using mind maps, spider diagrams or flash cards.
- Track your progress using the revision planner and give yourself a reward when you have achieved your target.

REVISED ☐

1 week to go

- Try to fit in at least one more timed practice of an entire past paper and seek feedback from your teacher, comparing your work closely with the mark scheme.
- Check the revision planner to make sure you haven't missed out any topics. Brush up on any areas of difficulty by talking them over with a friend or getting help from your teacher.
- Attend any revision classes put on by your teacher. Remember, he or she is an expert at preparing students for examinations.

REVISED ☐

The day before the examination

- Flick through these Revision Notes for useful reminders, for example the exam tips, exam summaries, typical mistakes and key terms.
- Check the time and place of your examination.
- Make sure you have everything you need — extra pens and pencils, tissues, a watch, bottled water, sweets.
- Allow some time to relax and have an early night to ensure you are fresh and alert for the examinations.

REVISED ☐

My exams

GCSE (9–1) Economics Paper 1
Date:..
Time:..
Location:..

GCSE (9–1) Economics Paper 2
Date:..
Time:..
Location:..

1 Main economic groups and factors of production

Main economic groups

- The three main economic groups are **consumers**, **producers** and **government**.
- Each group has different objectives that influence its behaviour.
- Each group's actions impact the economy through buying, producing or intervening in markets.
- **Goods** and **services** are terms that are used to differentiate two types of what can be bought and sold.

Consumers   REVISED

- Consumers are the buyers of goods and services.
- They are influenced by how much benefit they will gain from a good.
- This enables consumers to put a price on how much they value it.
- To make sensible decisions on the value of a good, consumers need to have information about the goods available and the ability to understand this information.

Producers   REVISED

- Producers are the sellers of goods and services.
- They are influenced by how much benefit they receive from a good.
- One benefit is **profit**.
- In order to maximise profit, suppliers choose what and how they produce.
- This can affect the quantity, price or quality of the goods produced.

Government   REVISED

- A government is a group of people who have the power to run a country.
- They are influenced by wanting the best for society.
- The government can impact the whole economy by its policies, e.g. changing the level of unemployment benefit.
- The government can impact markets for specific goods and services, e.g. by adding taxes.
- Governments spend money in an economy, e.g. providing services, such as healthcare, and transferring money directly to individuals, such as child benefit.

Consumer A person or organisation that directly uses a good or service.

Producer A person, company or country that makes, grows or supplies goods and/or services.

Government A political authority that decides how a country is run and manages its operation.

Good A tangible product, i.e. a product that can be seen or touched.

Service An intangible product, i.e. a product that cannot be seen or touched.

Exam tip

It is important to learn about key factors that influence consumers when valuing goods. It is also useful for evaluation to consider whether they are really able to make decisions that will maximise their benefits.

Profit The amount of money a producer has left after all costs have been paid.

Interdependence

REVISED

- There is interdependence between consumers, producers and government.
- This means the economic actions of one group are likely to impact another.
- This linking between the different groups is a key area to consider when thinking about what might happen after any change in an economy.

Now test yourself

TESTED

Identify which of the following are true or false:
1 An individual consumer's decision to consume alcohol does not have an impact on the government.
2 Consumers are influenced by how much profit they make when making economic decisions.
3 The government's decision to promote healthy eating can have an impact on producers of food.
4 The National Health Service is an example of a producer.
5 Travel insurance is an example of a good.

Answers online

> **Exam tip**
>
> Chains of reasoning are needed for higher-mark questions. These are a series of links that show clearly how something leads to something else. Practise this with different types of government intervention.

Factors of production

There are four key **factors of production** that affect the quantity and quality of output:
1 **Land** includes all raw materials that are naturally occurring, e.g. oil, trees, the sea and soil.
2 **Labour**: the workforce. It is affected by the quantity and quality of people able to work. The quality of the workforce is particularly affected by education and health.
3 **Capital** includes different types of machines and infrastructure, e.g. roads that are used during the manufacture of other goods and services.
4 **Enterprise**: this function is performed by entrepreneurs. They organise the other factors of production to create goods and services and bear the risks of the production process.

> **Factors of production** The resources in an economy that can be used to make goods and services, e.g. land, labour, capital and enterprise.
>
> **Land** The natural resources available for production in an economy.
>
> **Capital** The man-made aids to production in an economy.
>
> **Labour** The workforce available for production in an economy.
>
> **Enterprise** The factor of production that involves taking a risk and organising the other three factors in production.

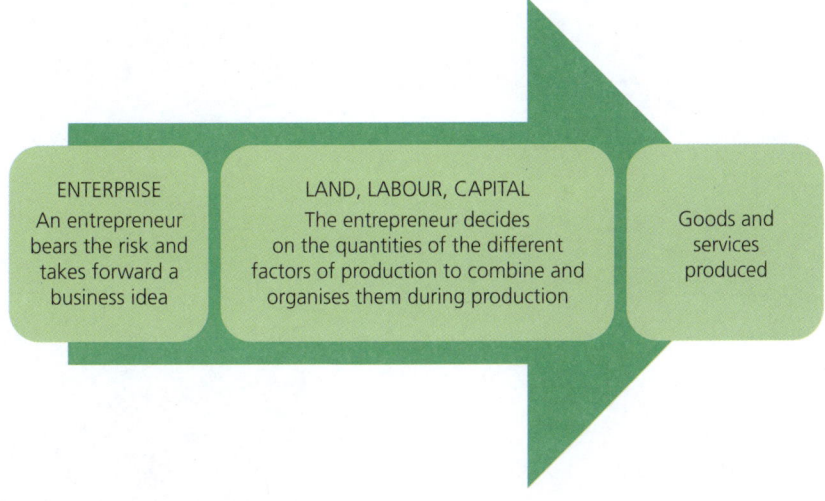

Figure 1.1 **The combination of factors of production and the production process**

> **Exam tip**
>
> Stress and apply the key characteristics of entrepreneurs when using an example. This can make an answer stronger and safer, especially when there is any overlap with labour.

OCR GCSE (9–1) Economics

Now test yourself

TESTED

Identify the factor of production for the following examples:
6. aeroplane
7. corner shop owner
8. runway
9. coal
10. warehouse

Answers online

Typical mistake
Use the definitions of the different factors of production as checklists for categorising examples. This can help avoid mistakes such as identifying buildings as land.

Exam practice

1. Which one of the following is **not** an example of land?
   A water
   B trees
   C air
   D petrol [1]
2. Which one of the following describes best the key motivation for firms?
   A the ability to maximise satisfaction from production of a good or service
   B the ability to maximise profit from production of a good or service
   C the ability to maximise the welfare of society from production of a good or service
   D the ability to maximise sales from production of a good or service [1]
3. State two types of the factors of production. [2]

Answers and quick quiz 1 online

ONLINE

Summary

You should have an understanding of:
- the three main economic groups of consumers, producers and the government
- the difference between goods and services
- the interdependence of consumers, producers and the government
- the four factors of production: land, labour, capital and enterprise
- the way the factors of production are combined to produce goods and services

2 The basic economic problem

Scarce resources and unlimited wants

- The **economic problem** is that there are **unlimited wants** for goods and services but there are only **scarce resources** to make them.
- Unlimited wants describes the desire that consumers could have for an infinite amount of goods if they had no limits such as affordability.
- Scarce resources are where there are a limited amount of factors of production available. This restricts which goods can be made.
- There are too many competing uses for the amount of resources available.

Economic problem How to best use limited resources to satisfy the unlimited wants of people.

Unlimited wants The infinite desire for something.

Scarce resources When there is an insufficient amount of something to satisfy all wants.

How, what and for whom

Economists think of ways to reduce the gap between what can be made and what is wanted by consumers. Three key questions are a starting point for reducing the economic problem:

1. How should goods and services be produced? For example, should firms use more technology, have large-scale production, or use incentives to motivate managers?
2. What should be produced? For example, should resources be used to make fizzy drinks, machines or hospitals?
3. For whom should the goods and services be produced? For example, should consumers only have goods they can afford to buy or are there goods that should be provided by the government for everyone?

Typical mistake

Take care not to confuse the word 'needs' with the idea of unlimited wants. 'Needs' are goods and services required for survival. There is only a limited list of needs, and it is possible that they could be fulfilled.

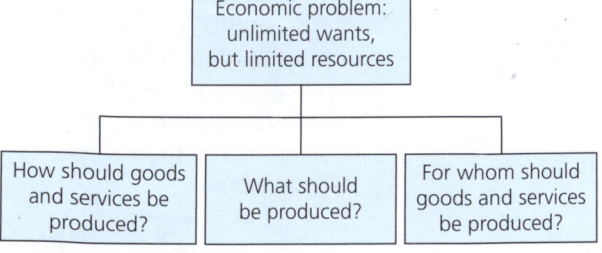

Figure 2.1 The economic problem and three key questions

Opportunity cost

- Once a decision is made on a use for scarce resources, then other options for their use are sacrificed.
- Opportunity cost is the term to describe what has been given up.
- It covers the missed benefits that the other options may have given to consumers.
- It can be used to compare what could have been gained from different uses of resources.
- It can help decide which goods and services should be produced.

Exam tip

Make it clear in your answers exactly what is the opportunity cost by linking the term with the example used. For example, a firm's choice to make more shampoo means it has to reduce the amount of soap it makes. The amount of soap given up is the opportunity cost.

Opportunity cost The next best alternative given up when making a choice.

OCR GCSE (9-1) Economics

Now test yourself

TESTED

Match the terms with the correct explanation.

1	Economic problem	B	A	The infinite desire for something
2	Opportunity cost	C	B	How to best use limited resources to satisfy the unlimited want
3	Scarce resources	D	C	Next best alternative given up when making a choice
4	Unlimited wants	A	D	An insufficient amount of something to satisfy all wants

Answers online

Costs and benefits of economic choices

- Economists weigh up the costs and benefits of different **economic choices**.
- This evaluation can help decide on the most beneficial use of resources for society.
- If costs of a good are greater than its benefits, then this would be a poor use of an economy's resources and production should be reduced.
- If benefits of a good are greater than its costs, then this would suggest that more should be made so that society can benefit.
- Economists consider the direct costs and benefits of different economic choices for consumers and producers.
- They also consider the side effects of goods and services that can impact society beyond the consumers and producers.

Economic, social and environmental sustainability

- Sustainability looks at the costs and benefits of economic choices both now and in the future.
- This enables economic decisions that can prioritise the use of scarce resources and help improve quality of life now without reducing it for future generations.
- Actions aimed at achieving one type of sustainability may have an impact on another type of sustainability, e.g. subsidising renewable energy may have a positive impact on the environment as well as economic benefits due to job creation.

Economic choice An option for the use of selected scarce resources.

Economic sustainability The best use of resources in order to create responsible development or growth, now and into the future.

Social sustainability The impact of development or growth that promotes an improvement in quality of life for all, now and into the future.

Environmental sustainability The impact of development or growth where the effect on the environment is small and possible to manage, now and into the future.

Exam tip

A question that asks you to *evaluate* includes marks for:
- Application: use of evidence from extracts and specific markets.
- Analysis: chains of reasoning to explain how theory works for the question set.
- Evaluation: weighing up of analysis, e.g. problems with theory or factors that offset.
- Judgement: overall answer to the question with brief support, e.g. that adds to, or prioritises, the arguments made.

Economic sustainability

REVISED

- Economic sustainability means that decisions are made that make financial sense for both now and the future.
- It should lead to growth or development for economies or enable firms to stay in business in the future.
- It can take into account all the economic costs and benefits of a good now and into the future.
- Examples of economic costs include:
  - costs of production, such as raw materials,
  - the price of the good that consumers pay
  - other reduced costs due to the economic choice, such as a choice that reduces unemployment and therefore benefit payments
- Examples of economic benefits include:
  - potential sales and profits over time
  - any financial benefits that result from the economic choice, such as spending on research that can lead to more innovative products that could lead to future sales

Social sustainability

REVISED

- Social sustainability means that decisions are made that improve a society's quality of life and wellbeing.
- It means that growth or development should meet the basic needs of all, now and into the future.
- It encourages fairness and a better society with respect for others and their quality of life, e.g the impact of an economic choice regarding transport provision considers access to leisure and services for groups in society, such as the elderly.
- A happier society may lead to a more productive economy over time.

Environmental sustainability

REVISED

- Environmental sustainability means that our environment is protected so that the earth can support humans and trade now and in the future.
- Choices may be prioritised that minimise harm to the environment over time.
- It includes consideration of the impact of:
  - use of renewable resources, such as using wood from managed forests, which can mean a continued source of a raw material as well as other environmental benefits
  - use of non-renewable resources, such as depletion of fossil fuels so all production is more difficult in the future
  - actions resulting in different types of pollution and potential climate change, such as air pollution and breathing problems for children

> **Exam tip**
>
> Starting points for evaluation may include:
> - **T**ime: how long might it last; how long does it take for an impact to occur?
> - **O**ther factors: might other changes offset the impact? Are there costs or benefits – which is greater?
> - **E**lasticity or **E**vidence: is price elasticity of demand relevant? (See Chapter 4 to review elasticity of demand.) Might estimates be wrong? Is there any relevant evidence?
> - **S**ize or **S**ignificance: how big is the change? How big is the final impact likely to be?

Exam practice

1. An opportunity cost of a consumer buying a chocolate bar could be:
   A the price of the chocolate bar
   B the calories from the chocolate bar
   C the benefits from buying an apple instead
   D the cost of producing an apple [1]
2. A country can make the following combinations of TVs and washing machines.

Output of TVs (millions)	Output of washing machines (millions)
5	21
10	20
20	18

   Which of the following would be the opportunity cost of increasing production of TVs from 5 to 10 million?
   A 10 million units of TVs
   B 21 million units of washing machines
   C 5 million units of TVs
   D 1 million units of washing machines [1]
3. Explain what is meant by economic choices that promote 'environmental sustainability'. [2]
4. Ellie and Will run a coffee shop. State one likely cost and one likely benefit of running this business. [2]

Answers and quick quiz 2 online

ONLINE

Summary

You should have an understanding of:
- the basic economic problem of scarce resources but unlimited wants
- the three key questions used in considering the economic problem: *how*, *what* and *for whom*
- the idea of opportunity cost when making economic choices
- the way economists weigh up costs and benefits of economic choices to evaluate their impact
- the impact of economic choices on economic, social and environmental sustainability

3 The role of markets

What is a market?

- A **market** is a way of bringing together buyers and sellers. Below are the main forms.

Type of Market	How it operates
Physical	Many stallholders either outside or under cover
Shop	Interaction between shopkeeper/assistant and customer
Auction	Price is set by the buyers in competition with each other
From home	Through internet or phone or catalogues

- A **market economy** works through the forces of demand and supply (see Chapters 4, 5 and 6) to determine how scarce resources (see Chapter 2) are allocated.

Primary, secondary and tertiary sectors

Sector	Activities involved in the sector
Primary	Agriculture, fishing, farming, forestry, mining, oil and gas extraction, quarrying
Secondary	Manufacturing: uses raw materials to make goods or parts to go into other goods
	Construction of buildings (e.g. houses) and infrastructure (e.g. roads)
Tertiary	Transport, retailing, entertainment, tourism, finance, media, health, education, government

Difference between the production of goods and services

REVISED

- **Production of goods** involves using raw materials and/or semi-finished goods to make a whole good. It is what is commonly called manufacturing.
- **Production of services** is the process of providing a service to a consumer.

> **Market** A way of bringing together buyers and sellers to buy and sell goods and services.
>
> **Market economy** An economy in which scarce resources are allocated by the market forces of supply and demand.

> **Primary sector** The direct use of natural resources including extraction of basic materials and goods from land and sea.
>
> **Secondary sector** All activities in an economy concerned with either manufacturing or construction.
>
> **Tertiary sector** All activities in an economy that involve the idea of service.

> **Typical mistake**
>
> Construction is part of the secondary sector **not** the tertiary sector. This is because building is a production process and *not* a service.

OCR GCSE (9-1) Economics 17

> **Now test yourself** TESTED
>
> Which of the following are examples of the tertiary sector?
> 1 accountancy
> 2 bankers
> 3 bridge building
> 4 growing apples
> 5 lawyers
> 6 refuse collection
>
> **Answers online**

Factor and product markets

The **product market** deals with goods and services while the **factor market** is concerned with the factors of production.

Factor markets   REVISED

This is where the services of the factors of production (see Chapter 1) are bought and sold, e.g. the skills of labour or the ability to take risk of enterprise (see Chapter 1).

The key ideas are:
- involves the buying and selling of the services of the factors of production
- the price of factors is decided by the interaction of demand and supply
- demand for the factors depends on the demand for the good or service produced
- households supply labour in return for wages/salaries

Product markets   REVISED

This is where final goods and services are offered for sale and bought by consumers, businesses and the public sector.

The key ideas are:
- buying and selling of final goods and services
- households, other firms and the public sector are the buyers
- prices are determined by the intersection of supply and demand for the good or service

Interdependence of factor and product markets

- In the factor market households are the owners of the factors of production. They sell these to firms (see the bottom half of Figure 3.1).
- In the product market households are the main buyers of goods and services while firms are the sellers of these goods and services (see top half of Figure 3.1).

Product market Where final goods and services are offered to consumers, businesses and the public sector.

Factor market Where the services of the factors of production are bought and sold.

Typical mistake

Actual factors are **not** sold in factor markets, but what the factors offer can be sold, such as suitability of the land, or skills of the workforce such as computing.

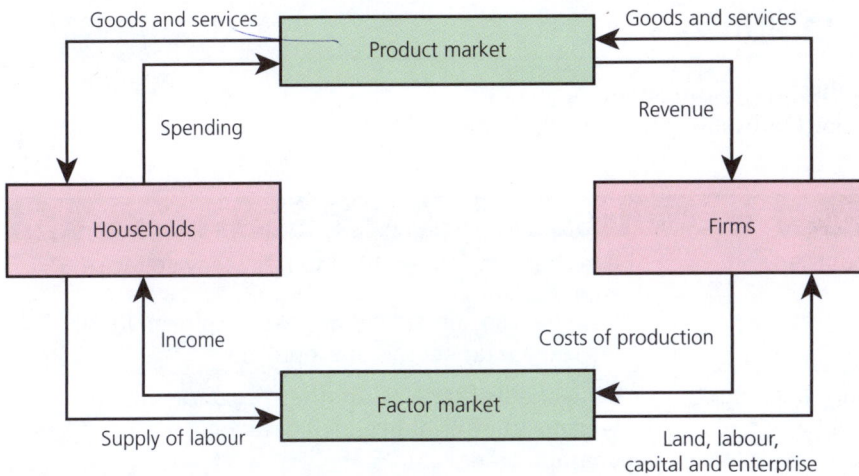

Figure 3.1 The relationship between factor and product markets

Specialisation and exchange

Specialisation and **exchange** can have benefits and costs for producers, workers, regions and countries.

> **Specialisation** The process by which individuals, firms, regions and countries concentrate on producing those products that they are best at doing.
>
> **Exchange** The giving up of something that an individual or firm has in return for something they wish to have, but do not possess.

Costs and benefits for producers

REVISED

Specialisation allows producers to gain economies of scale (see Chapter 8).

Benefits for producers	Costs for producers
Higher output: total production of goods and services is increased	Diseconomies of scale: as output increases costs may eventually rise
Higher productivity: as workers become more skilled	If one part of the process fails then the whole production system may stop
Higher quality: as the best factors can be employed	May not be able to buy necessary scarce resources or components
Bigger market for each product means there should be more buyers for each producer	Movement of workers: workers may become bored and leave or produce less
Economies of scale: larger output enables these to be gained	
Specialisation saves time and money	

Costs and benefits for workers

REVISED

Specialisation by individuals within a work place is called *division of labour*.

Benefits for workers	Costs for workers
Increased skill so may earn more	Boredom: leading to demotivation
Workers are able to do what they are best at, again allowing them to earn more	Deskilling: workers are unable to do different jobs so are less able to respond to changes
Increased job satisfaction: doing what they're good at increases motivation and satisfaction	Unemployment – see Chapter 12 – and may be easier to replace them with machines
Increased standard of living by earning more	

OCR GCSE (9-1) Economics   19

Costs and benefits for regions

REVISED

Regions within a country can specialise, e.g. Cumberland sausages from Cumbria and Stilton cheese from Derbyshire, Leicestershire and Nottinghamshire.

Benefits for regions	Costs for regions
A region makes best use of its resources	If demand falls then the industry may collapse
Creates jobs for residents near to home	If resources run out then those employed in the industry will become unemployed
Development of better infrastructure and supply industries	Loss of advantage as another region/country becomes better at producing, leading to unemployment

Costs and benefits for countries

REVISED

Specialisation by countries leads to international trade with exports of the specialist products and imports of those of other countries.

Benefits for countries	Costs for countries
Countries will specialise in what they do best, leading to greater efficiency and output	As specialisation changes, workers in the declining industry become unemployed
More jobs: the increased output may result in more investment and job creation	Over-specialisation: if world demand changes the economy may collapse
International trade of the surplus output and greater choice of products for its people	Increased output leading to over-exploiting resources so unsustainable development
Increased choice, income, output and infrastructure gives a better standard of living	Negative externalities can lead to serious environmental damage
Government revenue increases leading to better schools, hospitals etc.	

Exam practice

1. An example of a tertiary sector activity is:
   A building a new house
   B producing mobile phones
   C quarrying slate
   D transporting goods to shops [1]
2. Explain the difference between a factor and a product market. [2]
3. Evaluate the costs and benefits of specialisation for a country. [6]

Answers and quick quiz 3 online

ONLINE

Summary

You should have an understanding of:
- what is meant by a market
- different types of markets
- what types of industries form the primary sector
- what types of industries form the secondary sector
- what types of industries form the tertiary sector
- the difference between the production of goods and services
- the difference between factor and product markets
- the interdependence of factor and product markets
- the costs and benefits of specialisation for producers, workers, regions and countries
- how to evaluate each of these costs and benefits

Answers and quick quizzes at www.hoddereducation.co.uk/myrevisionnotesdownloads

4 Demand

What is meant by demand?

- **Demand** must be effective to be demand in economics.
- Effective demand means that the consumer *both* wants to buy the product *and* has the money to do so.
- Just wanting the product is *not* demand.
- Demand may also depend on the demand for another product. An example would be: demand for popcorn at the cinema depends on demand for cinema tickets/seats.

Price, quantity and demand

- For most products the quantity demanded and the price move in opposite directions.
- This inverse relationship is called the **law of demand**.
- As price falls more people can afford the product so quantity demanded increases.
- As price falls people spend less money on the product so can afford to buy more.

> **Demand** The willingness and ability to purchase a good or service at the given price in a given time period.
>
> **Law of demand** Normally, the quantity demanded varies inversely with the price.

Drawing and explaining a demand curve

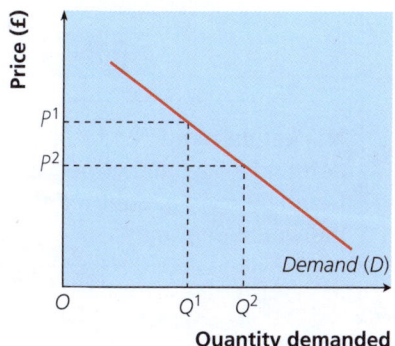

Figure 4.1 The demand curve

In nearly all cases the demand curve slopes downwards.
- If asked to draw a demand curve in the exam it is most likely to slope downwards.
- Remember to label the axes P (price) and Q (quantity), and the demand curve D (demand).

Now test yourself

TESTED

1 Use the information in the table to draw a demand curve.

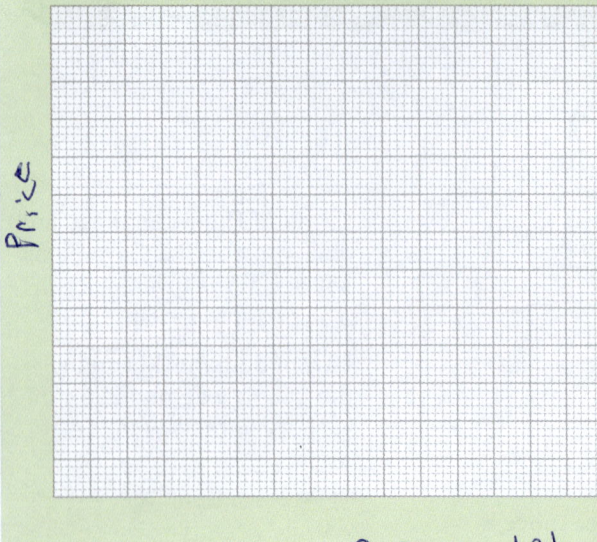

Price (p)	Quantity demanded
30	4
25	8
20	12
15	16
10	20
5	24

Answers online

Individual demand

REVISED

Each individual consumer will have his/her own demand curve for a product. This is known as **individual demand**.

An individual's demand schedule (such as in the 'Now test yourself' example) shows us how much that person will buy at each price. It *does not show the actual amount bought* as we do not know anything about supply.

Individual demand The demand for a good or service by an individual consumer.

Market demand

REVISED

The total demand for a product in a market is called the **market demand**. To get this the individual demand schedules of all consumers must be added together.

Market demand The total demand for a good or service found by adding together all individual demands.

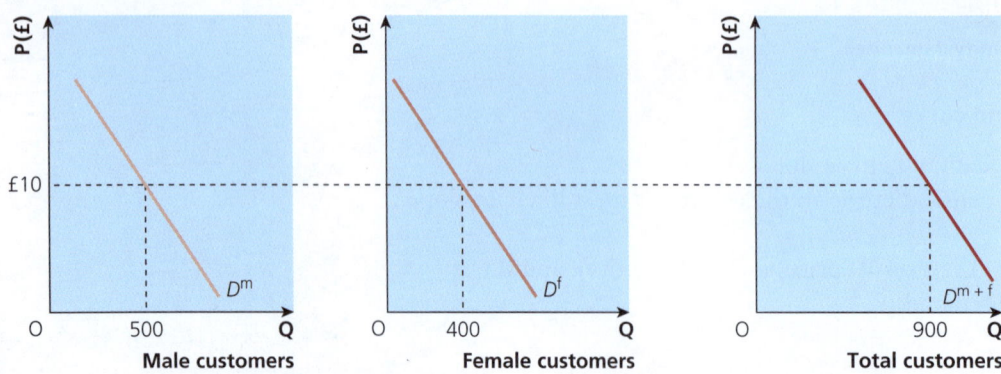

Figure 4.2 The market demand curve

Explaining a demand curve

REVISED

An explanation of a **demand curve** involves:
- a definition: a graph showing how the demand for a commodity or service varies with changes in its price
- a statement that normally price and quantity have an inverse relationship

> **Demand curve** A graph showing how the demand for a product varies with changes in its price.
>
> **Shift of the demand curve** A complete movement of the existing demand curve either outward, to the right, or inward, to the left.
>
> **Movement along the demand curve** When the price changes (due to a change in supply) leading to a movement up or down the existing demand curve.

Drawing shifts of, and movements along, the demand curve

It is very important to distinguish between a **shift of the demand curve**, which means the whole curve moves inwards or outwards, and a **movement along the demand curve**, which means going up or down the curve.

Shifts of the demand curve

REVISED

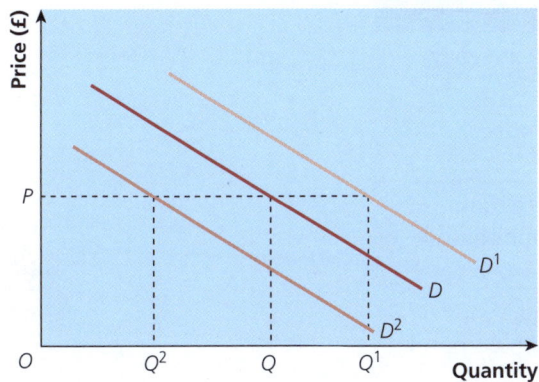

Figure 4.3 Shift of the demand curve

Shifts in the demand curve are caused by *non-price factors* (see below).

Now test yourself

TESTED

2 Using the demand curve diagram you drew for the previous 'Now test yourself' question, draw a new demand curve to show what would happen if the demand doubles at each price.

Answers online

Movements along the demand curve

REVISED

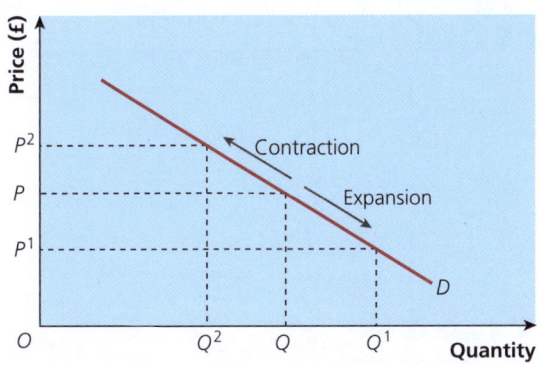

Figure 4.4 Movement along the demand curve

> **Typical mistake**
>
> A common error is to confuse a movement/shift of the demand curve with a movement along the demand curve. Make sure you are clear about the differences.

OCR GCSE (9–1) Economics 23

- A movement up the demand curve is a contraction in demand.
- A movement down the demand curve is an expansion in demand.
- NB *both of these are the result of a shift in the supply curve* (see Chapter 5).

Causes and consequences of shifts of, and movements along, the demand curve

> **Exam tip**
>
> When the exam question asks you to *analyse*, you should demonstrate the ability to present logical chains of reasoning based on knowledge and application. It involves the use of economic terms and the explanation of diagrams.

- A shift of a demand curve is caused by non-price factors.
- A movement along the demand curve is a result of a change in price only.

Causes of shifts of the demand curve

REVISED

The table includes causes which would shift the demand curve. The effects of shifting it (increase) are considered. A movement to the left (decrease) would have the opposite effects.

Cause	Effect
Increase in income	Consumers can buy more products at every price
Increase in marketing (advertising)	Persuades consumers to demand more products at every price
Change in taste and fashion	If people prefer smartphones to notebook computers, then demand for smartphones increases
Preference for a substitute	If honey and jam are substitutes and consumers decide to use honey, then demand for it will increase
Complementary goods	If the price of one good falls, then demand for any good which goes with it (e.g. petrol and cars) will increase
Expectation of a rise in price	Consumers will buy more products now to save money in the future
Population changes	- If population rises so does demand for products - If the population is ageing, demand for goods suited to older people will increase - Gender working patterns, e.g. more women working, increases demand for nursery places for children
Government policies	A **subsidy** or a cut in **tax** will increase consumers' demand

> **Subsidy** An amount of money a government gives directly to firms to encourage production and consumption.
>
> **Tax** A compulsory payment to the government.

Consequences of shifts of the demand curve

REVISED

In nearly all situations this will result in price and quantity moving in the *same direction*.

Change in demand	Change in price	Change in quantity
Increases/moves to the right	Rises	Rises
Decreases/moves to the left	Falls	Falls

Note the following exceptions:
- If incomes rise faster than prices, then consumers can demand more.
- If a substitute is preferred, then demand will fall even if price falls.
- If the increase in demand allows firms to gain economies of scale (see Chapter 8), then they could cut prices leading to an extension of demand.
- If demand falls a firm could go out of business.

Causes of movements along the demand curve

REVISED

A movement along the demand curve is caused *solely* by a change in price/supply (see Chapters 5 and 6).

Consequences of movements along the demand curve

REVISED

Price and quantity move in *opposite* directions.

Change in price	Change in quantity	Effect on consumers	Effect on firms
Rise	Fall	Buy fewer goods	Sales fall as do profits
		Buy cheaper substitutes	May need fewer workers
Fall	Rise	Buy more and better goods	Increase supply and profit
			Employ more workers

Now test yourself
TESTED

3 i) If there is an extension of supply this means that price has .... and quantity has ....
   ii) If supply has decreased this means that price has .... and quantity has ....

Answers online

Price elasticity of demand The responsiveness of quantity demanded to a change in the price of the product.

Elastic demand When the percentage change in quantity demanded is greater than the percentage change in price.

Inelastic demand When the percentage change in quantity demanded is less than the percentage change in price.

Price elasticity of demand

The demand curve tells us that if price falls, quantity demanded increases. **Price elasticity of demand** (PED) tells us, however, by how much quantity demanded will change in response to a change in price.

Value of PED	Meaning of the value
0	There is no change in quantity as price changes
Between 0 and −1	Change in quantity is less than the change in price
−1	Change in quantity is equal to the change in price
Between 0 and ∞	Change in quantity is more than the change in price
∞ (infinity)	An infinite amount can be demanded at the given price: no change in price

> **Exam tip**
>
> Always include the minus (−) sign in your answer for PED. This shows that the demand curve slopes downwards.

Drawing demand curves of different elasticity

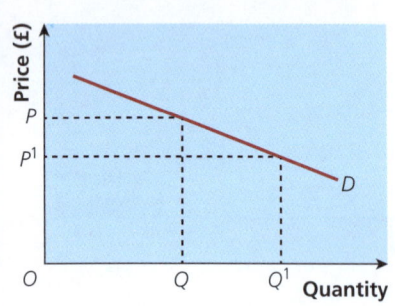

Figure 4.5 Price elastic demand curve

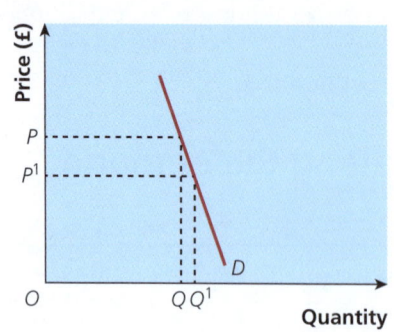

Figure 4.6 Price inelastic demand curve

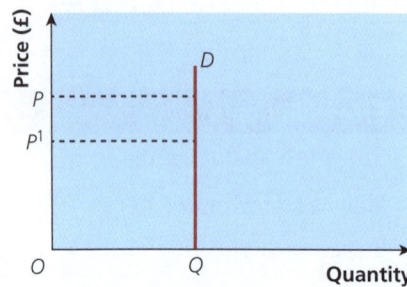

Figure 4.7 Perfectly price inelastic demand curve

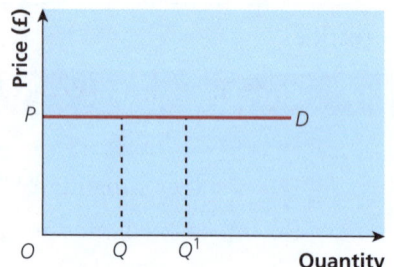

Figure 4.8 Perfectly price elastic demand curve

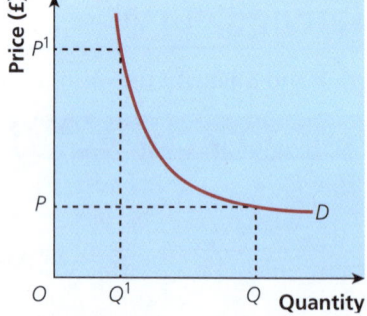

Figure 4.9 Unitary price elastic demand curve

You should refer to the table above while studying these demand curves.

For a straight-line demand curve, demand changes all the way along.

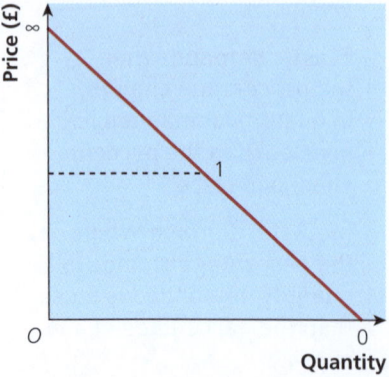

Figure 4.10 How elasticity varies along the demand curve

26 Answers and quick quizzes at www.hoddereducation.co.uk/myrevisionnotesdownloads

The importance of price elasticity of demand

PED allows consumers and producers to know what the effect of a change in demand or price will be.

The importance of price elasticity of demand for consumers

REVISED

- If the product they buy has inelastic demand then they are likely to face price rises as suppliers can easily pass on cost increases.
- If the product they buy has inelastic demand then the government can impose high taxes raising prices.
- Allows them to make choices if substitutes are available.
- Consumers PED may depend on factors such as the weather/time of the year or day.

The importance of price elasticity of demand for producers

REVISED

- allows producers to maximise their total revenue (see Chapter 8)
- can charge different prices to different groups of people for the same product
- can affect their decision whether to supply the product or not to

Exam practice

1 The cause of an extension in demand for television sets is a:
   A fall in the population
   B fall in the price
   C rise in number of substitutes
   D rise in taxation [1]
2 Evaluate the importance of price elasticity of demand for railway companies. [6]

Answers and quick quiz 4 online

ONLINE

Summary

You should have an understanding of:
- what is meant by demand
- how to draw demand curves for individuals and the market
- how to explain these demand curves
- what is meant by a shift of, and a movement along, the demand curve
- how to draw shifts of, and movements along, the demand curve
- analysing the causes and effects of these shifts and movements for consumers
- analysing the causes and effects of these shifts and movements for producers
- what is meant by price elasticity of demand
- how to draw demand curves of different elasticities
- how to evaluate the importance of price elasticity of demand for consumers and producers

5 Supply

What is meant by supply?

According to the **law of supply**, the **supply** curve slopes upwards, because:
- Firms are likely to gain higher profits by supplying more.
- Production costs are likely to rise as more is produced.
- This enables new firms to enter the market as they often have higher costs.

Time is a very important factor as it is easy to increase supply of some products 'in a given time period' but difficult for other products. More cornflakes, for example, can be supplied to shops relatively quickly. Wembley Stadium, however, seats 90,000 people. To supply more seats would take a long time.

> **Law of supply** Normally, the quantity supplied varies directly with the price.
>
> **Supply** The ability and willingness of firms to provide goods and services at each price in a given time period.

Drawing and explaining a supply curve

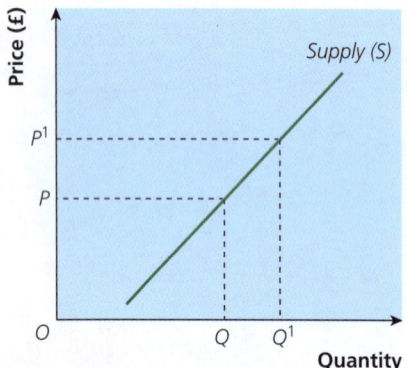

Figure 5.1 The supply curve

- If asked to draw a supply curve in the exam it is most likely to slope upwards.
- Remember to label the axes P (price) and Q (quantity), and the supply curve S (supply).

Explaining a supply curve

REVISED

An explanation of a **supply curve** involves:
- A definition: a graph showing how the supply of a commodity or service varies with changes in its price.
- A statement that normally price and quantity have a direct relationship.

> **Supply curve** A graph showing how the supply of a product varies with changes in its price.

Now test yourself

TESTED

1. Use the information in the table to draw a supply curve.

Price (p)	Quantity supplied
10	2
20	4
30	8
40	16
50	32
60	64

Answers online

Individual supply

REVISED

Each individual producer will have his/her own supply curve for a product. This is known as **individual supply**.

An individual's supply schedule (such as in the 'Now test yourself' example) shows us how much that producer will be prepared to sell at each price. It *does not show the actual amount supplied* as we do not know anything about demand.

Individual supply The supply of a good or service by an individual producer.

Market supply

REVISED

The total supply of a product in a market is called the **market supply**. To get this the individual supply schedules of all producers must be added together.

Market supply The total supply of a good or service found by adding together all individual producers' supplies.

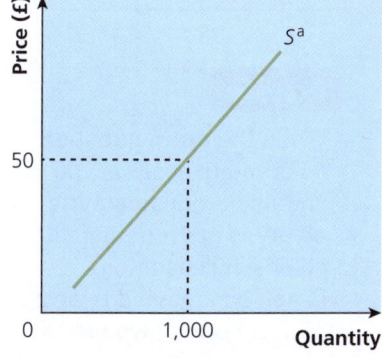
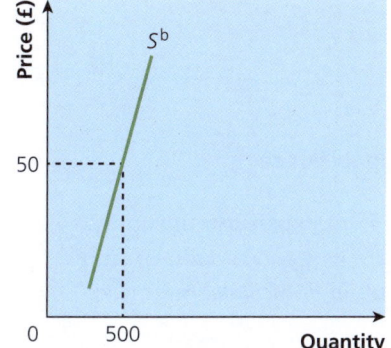
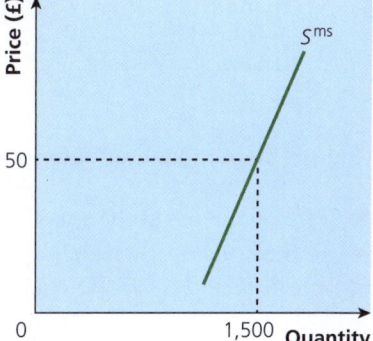

Figure 5.2 The market supply curve

OCR GCSE (9–1) Economics 29

Drawing shifts of, and movements along, the supply curve

It is very important to distinguish between a **shift of the supply curve**, which means the whole curve moves inwards or outwards, and a **movement along the supply curve**, which means going up or down the curve.

Shifts of the supply curve

REVISED

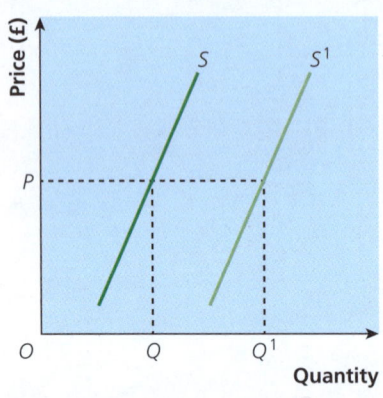

Figure 5.3 A shift of the supply curve

Shifts in the supply curve are caused by *non-price factors*, see below.

> **Shift of the supply curve** A complete movement of the existing supply curve either outward, to the right, or inward, to the left (showing either more or less is supplied at every price).
>
> **Movement along the supply curve** When the price changes (due to a change in demand) leading to a movement up or down the existing supply curve.

Now test yourself

TESTED

2 Use the supply curve you drew for the previous 'Now test yourself'. If the supply falls by 4 units at each price, draw a new supply curve.

Answers online

Movements along the supply curve

REVISED

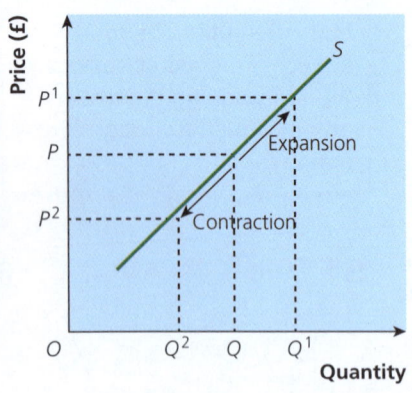

Figure 5.4 A movement along the supply curve

- A movement up the supply curve is an expansion in supply.
- A movement down the supply curve is a contraction in supply.
- NB both of these are the result of a shift in the demand curve (see Chapter 4).

> **Typical mistake**
>
> A common error is to confuse a movement/shift of the supply curve with a movement along the supply curve. Make sure you are clear about the differences.

> **Exam tip**
>
> When the exam question asks you to *analyse*, you should demonstrate the ability to present logical chains of reasoning based on knowledge and application. It involves the use of economic terms and the explanation of diagrams.

Causes and consequences of shifts of, and movements along, the supply curve

- A shift of a supply curve is caused by non-price factors.
- A movement along the supply curve is a result of a change in price only.

Causes of shifts of the supply curve

REVISED

The table includes the main causes which would shift the supply curve. Only either an increase or a decrease are considered.

Cause	Effect
Increase in costs of production	Producers would supply less at each price
Increase in taxes and subsidies (see Chapter 4)	Increase in indirect taxes (see Chapter 15) means a rise in costs. Increase in subsidies has the opposite effect
New technology	Is likely to lead to a fall in costs and thus a rightward shift
Climate change	In agriculture, climate warming may mean less can be supplied of a product
Increase in producers or size of firms	Both will lead to more being supplied at every price: a rightward shift
Government regulation	Introduction of new government regulations such as health and safety will increase costs leading to a shift to the left

Now test yourself

TESTED

3 Draw three diagrams to show what would happen to supply if: (i) costs of production fell; (ii) indirect taxes were reduced; and (iii) subsidies were reduced.

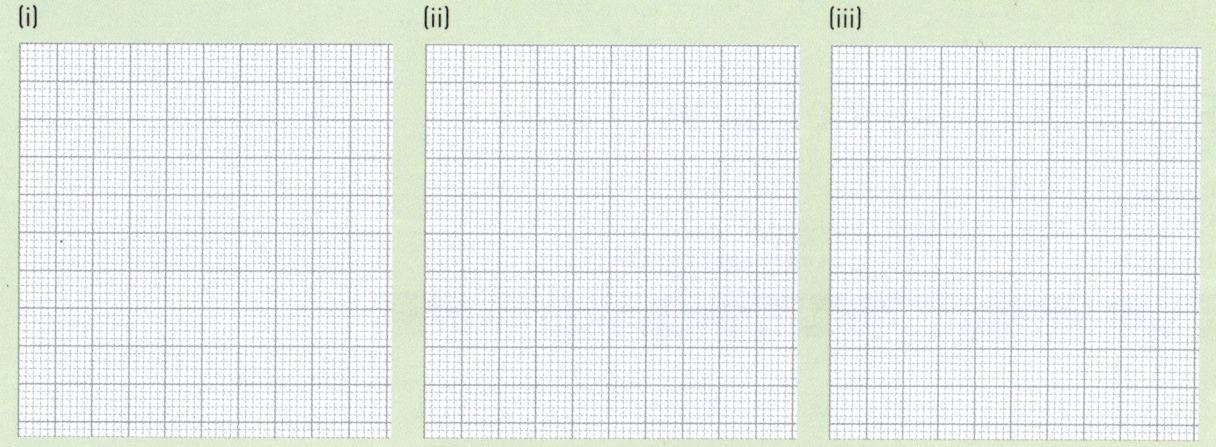

(i)   (ii)   (iii)

Answers online

Consequences of shifts of the supply curve

REVISED

In nearly all situations this will result in price and quantity moving in the *opposite direction*. Thus, if supply shifts to the right, price falls while quantity increases.

Consequence	Outcome
Can gain greater economies of scale (see Chapter 8)	Greater profits for the producer and/or lower prices for consumers
Increase in efficiency	Increase in profit and also possibly greater productivity (see Chapter 8)
Increase in sales	If price falls then consumers are likely to buy more leading to increase in profit
Increase in exports (see Chapter 19)	Greater economies of scale, increase in efficiency and fall in price makes the firm more competitive
Become a monopoly/oligopoly (see Chapter 7)	If a firm is more competitive it gains market share and forces competitors out

Causes of movements along the supply curve

REVISED

A movement along the supply curve is caused *solely* by a change in price/demand (see Chapters 4 and 6).

Consequences of movements along the supply curve

REVISED

Price and quantity move in the *same* direction.

Change in price	Change in quantity	Effect on producers	Effect on consumers
Rise	Rise	Initial increase in profits	Products are now more expensive
		More firms enter the market shifting supply to the right which might reduce profit	Price falls. Consumers have more choice and can now buy more products
Fall	Fall	Reduction in profits: less efficient firms forced out. Reduction in output	Consumers can afford more, but now have less choice

Price elasticity of supply

The supply curve tells us that if price rises, quantity increases. **Price elasticity of supply** (PES) tells us, however, by how much quantity supplied will change in response to a change in price.

Value of PED	Meaning of the value
0	There is no change in quantity as price changes
Between 0 and 1	Change in quantity is less than the change in price
1	Change in quantity is equal to the change in price
Between 0 and ∞	Change in quantity is more than the change in price
∞ (infinity)	An infinite amount can be supplied at the given price: no change in price

> **Price elasticity of supply** The responsiveness of quantity supplied to a change in the price of the product.
>
> **Elastic supply** When the percentage change in quantity supplied is greater than the percentage change in price.
>
> **Inelastic supply** When the percentage change in quantity supplied is less than the percentage change in price.

> **Exam tip**
>
> Remember that while PED needs a minus sign in front of the number (−), PES is positive so does not need any sign.

Drawing supply curves of different elasticity

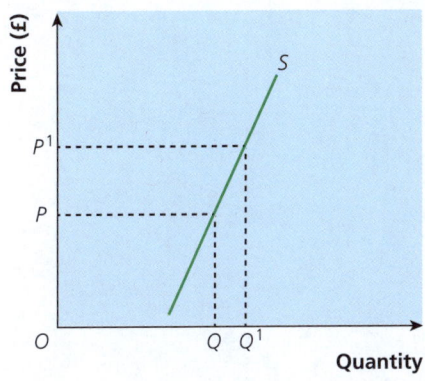
Figure 5.5 Price inelastic supply curve

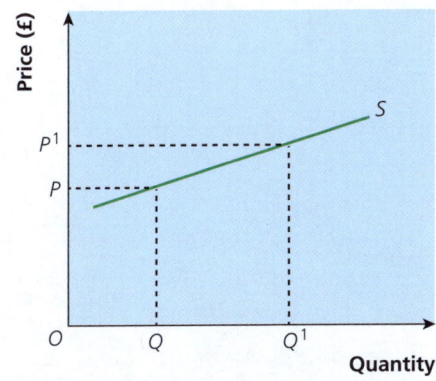
Figure 5.6 Price elastic supply curve

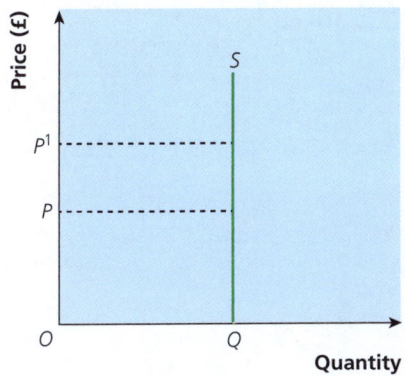
Figure 5.7 Perfectly price inelastic supply curve

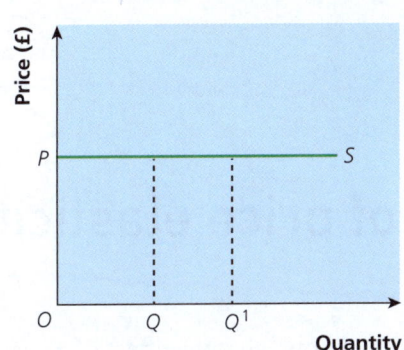
Figure 5.8 Perfectly price elastic supply curve

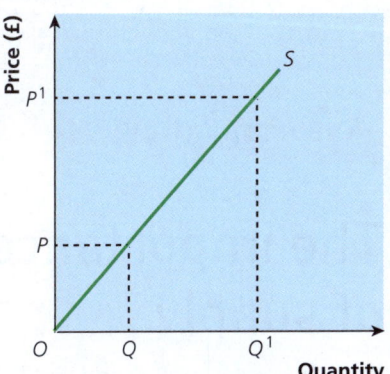
Figure 5.9 Unitary price elastic supply curve

You should refer to the table above while studying these supply curves.

Now test yourself

TESTED

4   You are told that Jesse supplies 10 bags at £10 each and 40 bags at £60 each, while Reema supplies 10 at £10 each but 80 bags at £60 each.
   i) Draw the two individual supply curves. Which is elastic and which inelastic?

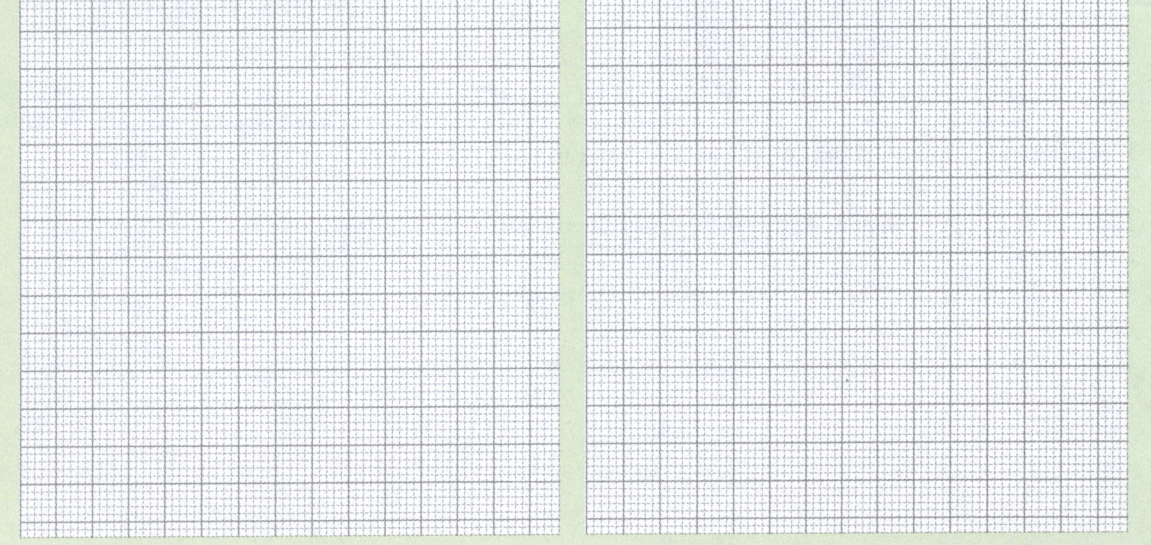

OCR GCSE (9–1) Economics

ii) Now draw the market supply curve. Is this elastic or inelastic?

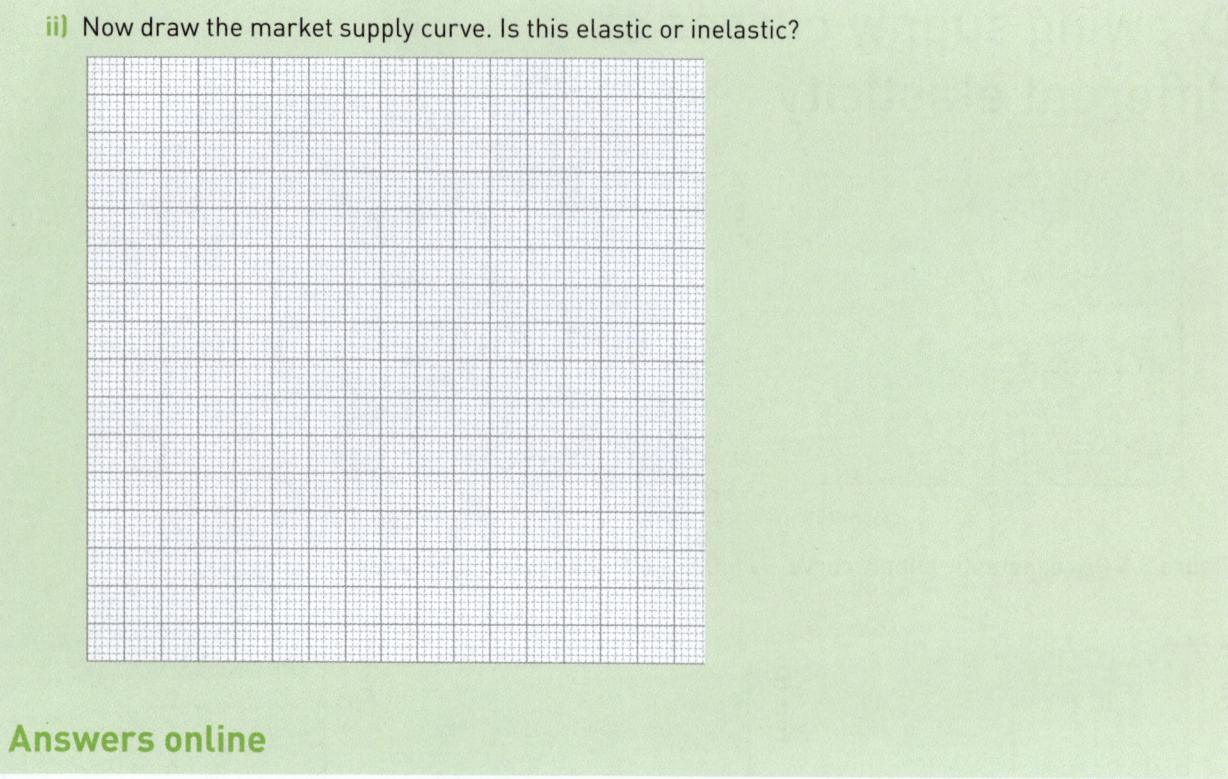

Answers online

The importance of price elasticity of supply

PES allows consumers and producers to know what the effect of a change in supply or price will be.

Price elasticity of supply for consumers

REVISED

- If the product consumers buy has inelastic supply, then they are likely to face high prices in order to obtain more.
- If the product they buy has a very inelastic supply, then they may not be able to get more as the quantity is fixed. This can give rise to ticket touts when demand exceeds supply.
- If the product they buy has an elastic supply then it is quite easy to purchase more.

Price elasticity of supply for producers

REVISED

- Firms would prefer an elastic supply as it is easier to respond to price changes.
- More elastic supply enables a firm to be more flexible in what it offers consumers.
- Very inelastic supply means that the price will depend entirely on the demand.
- Can lead to losing control of the price to ticket touts.

Exam practice

1. Price elasticity of supply measures:
   A change in quantity supplied responding to an expansion or contraction of supply
   B how quantity supply changes in relation to a change in price
   C the responsiveness of quantity supplied to a change in price
   D when the percentage change in quantity supplied is less than that of price [1]
2. Draw and label a diagram showing an extension of the supply curve. [2]
3. Evaluate the importance of price elasticity of supply for supermarkets. [6]

Answers and quick quiz 5 online

ONLINE

Summary

You should have an understanding of:
- what is meant by supply
- how to draw supply curves for individuals and the market
- how to explain these supply curves
- what is meant by a shift of, and a movement along, the supply curve
- how to draw shifts of, and movements along, the supply curve
- analysing the causes and effects of these shifts and movements for consumers
- analysing the causes and effects of these shifts and movements for producers
- what is meant by price elasticity of supply
- how to draw supply curves of different elasticities
- how to evaluate the importance of price elasticity of supply for consumers and producers

6 Price

Price as a reflection of worth and its role in determining an efficient distribution of resources

In a market economy, **price** is determined by the interaction of demand and supply (see last section of this chapter).

> **Price** The sum of money which has to be paid for a good or service.

Price as a reflection of worth   REVISED

- Price is used to indicate worth.
- Worth is how much you value something.
- Worth varies depending on fashion, differences between people, the situation etc.
- Individuals may all be prepared to pay a different price for a product, i.e. they value the product differently.
- Price and worth may be very similar where, for example, you are willing to pay a high price to get something you really want.

Role of price in determining efficient resource allocation   REVISED

If you are not sure about scarce resources refer to Chapter 2.
- Best production level is where average costs are lowest and profits are highest (see Chapter 7).
- Price is the means of allocating scarce resources between competing users.

Price function	How the price function works
Signalling	Prices signal where resources are needed. If the price rises, more resources are allocated to that area
Transmission of preference	By making choices producers indicate their needs. Again, higher prices encourage owners of resources to supply more to producers
Rationing	Where resources are scarce, price rises so that demand equals supply

Equilibrium price and quantity

- Equilibrium price is the market clearing price where the amount that producers wish to sell is exactly equal to the amount consumers wish to buy.
- This is efficient because there is no excess demand or supply.

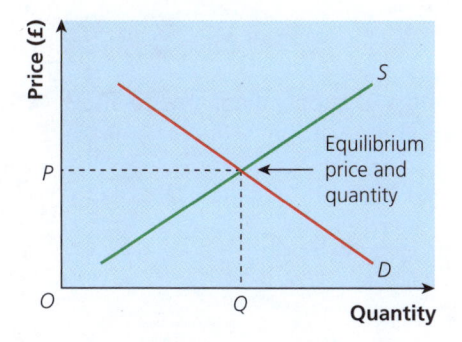

Figure 6.1 Equilibrium price and quantity

The diagram shows **equilibrium price** (OP) and **equilibrium quantity** (OQ).

> **Equilibrium price and quantity** Where the quantity supplied exactly matches the quantity demanded.

Drawing and analysing the interaction of demand and supply

Analysis can only take place if the diagrams are correct.

The interaction of demand and supply

REVISED

Before starting this section refer back to Chapters 4 and 5 about drawing demand and supply curves.

Example

Consumers' real incomes have increased. Draw a diagram to show this.

> **Exam tip**
>
> Check that you have: a downward sloping demand curve; an upward sloping supply curve; all lines and axes labelled correctly. If the diagram does not show the outcome you expect *check again*.

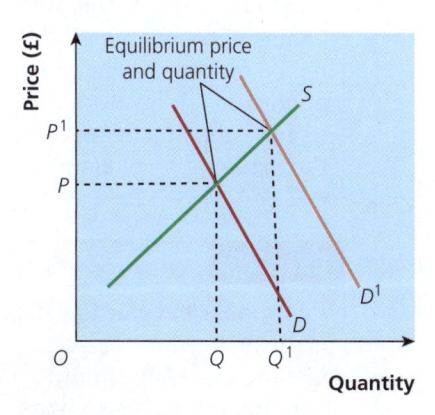

Figure 6.2 The effect of an increase in demand showing application of the technique of drawing supply and demand diagrams

Supply and demand curves are shown correctly and labelled, as are the axes. Original equilibrium is shown. Real income leads to an increase in demand so the demand curve is shifted to the right and the new equilibrium is shown.

OCR GCSE (9-1) Economics 37

Now test yourself

TESTED

1. The price of desktop computers is expected to rise. Draw two demand and supply diagrams to show two ways in which this could occur and the resulting effects on price and quantity.

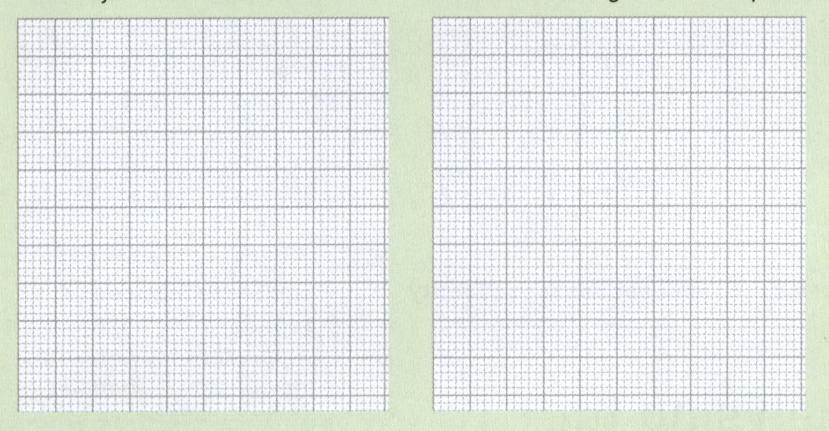

Answers online

Analysing the interaction of demand and supply

REVISED

This means using diagrams and economic terms and concepts to explain how demand and supply interact.

Example

Analyse the effect on consumers of smartphones of an increase in the number of producers.

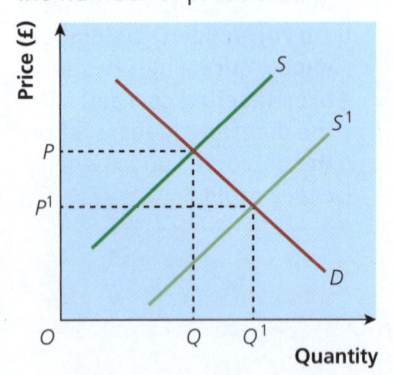

Figure 6.3 The effect of an increase in supply showing application of the technique of drawing supply and demand diagrams

The diagram shows that more producers has led to a shift in the supply curve from S to S^1. This has resulted in a fall in price from P to P^1 and an increase in quantity from Q to Q^1. Consumers now have to spend less to get a smartphone, which is likely to mean that more consumers will purchase one and those with a smartphone may now buy more than one or change their phone more often.

Exam tip

When the exam question asks you to *analyse*, you should demonstrate the ability to present logical chains of reasoning based on knowledge and application. It involves the use of economic terms and the explanation of diagrams.

Exam tip

Remember to refer to your diagram in your analysis. Instead of saying 'when demand increases so does price and quantity', say 'when demand increases from D to D^1 price rises from P to P^1 and quantity from Q to Q^1'.

The role of markets in the determination of price and the allocation of resources

If you are not sure about markets go back to Chapter 3.

The role of markets in the determination of price

REVISED

The **determination of price** is the interaction of the market forces of demand and supply to establish an equilibrium price.
- If the price is too high, demand is lower than supply leading to a fall in price until $D = S$ (excess supply).
- If the price is too low, then demand exceeds supply leading to a rise in price until $D = S$ (excess demand).
- Excess demand or supply leads to a disequilibrium.

Determination of price The interaction of the market forces of demand and supply to establish the general level of prices for a good or service.

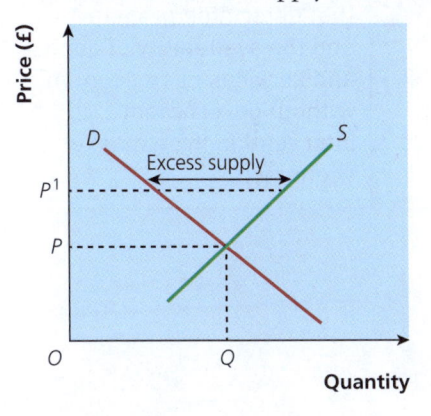

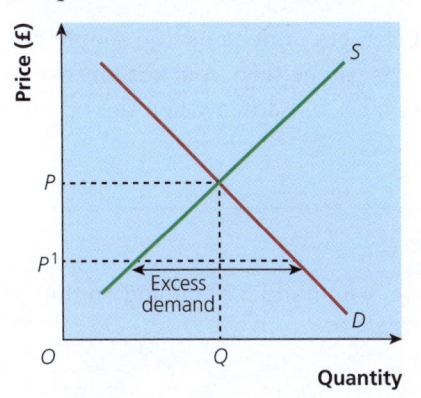

Figure 6.4 Excess supply

Figure 6.5 Excess demand

The role of markets in the allocation of resources

REVISED

In a market system, prices are the means for the **allocation of resources** (see Chapter 2 and above on excess supply and demand).

Stage 1
- Owners of factors of production sell their resources for the highest price to the highest bidder

Stage 2
- Firms buy the resources and produce goods and services to sell that people will buy (pay the price) in order to make profit

Stage 3
- Consumers buy goods and services which they most desire with their limited income gained from selling their resources

Allocation of resources How scarce resources are distributed among producers and how scarce goods and services are allocated among consumers.

Figure 6.6 Flow of resources

OCR GCSE (9–1) Economics 39

How the market forces of demand and supply affect equilibrium price and quantity

Table 6.1 Summary of changes in equilibrium price and quantity

Shift in demand	Effect on demand	Effect on equilibrium price	Effect on equilibrium quantity
To the right	Increases	Increases	Increases
To the left	Decreases	Decreases	Decreases

Shift in supply	Effect on supply	Effect on equilibrium price	Effect on equilibrium quantity
To the right	Increases	Decreases	Increases
To the left	Decreases	Increases	Decreases

Table 6.1 summarises the effects of changes in demand and supply on the equilibrium price and quantity. As can be seen, **market forces** push prices up when demand rises/supply falls, and down when the opposite occurs.

> **Market forces** The factors that determine price levels and the availability of goods and services in an economy without government intervention (free market economy).

Example

Analyse the effects of an increase in demand for housing on the equilibrium price of land in the UK.

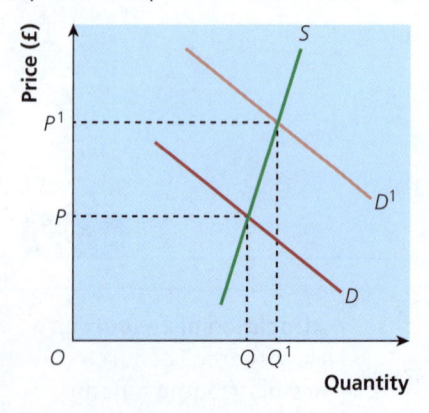

Figure 6.7 The effect of an increase in demand for land

The supply of land for housing is fairly inelastic (see Chapter 5). This is because not all land is suitable while the total supply of land in the UK is fixed. As a result, as demand rises from D to D^1, quantity supplied only increases by a small amount, Q to Q^1, but the price increases much more from P to P^1 giving a new equilibrium price and quantity of P^1Q^1.

> **Exam tip**
> In answering questions on demand and supply, price elasticity is normally worth considering as it may affect your answer.

Exam practice

1. Which of the following is the best way in which prices can help determine the distribution of resources?
   A create an equilibrium level of price and quantity
   B decide on the equilibrium level of quantity demanded
   C provide resource information to governments
   D signal to suppliers where resources are needed [1]

2. Using a diagram, explain what is meant by equilibrium price and quantity.

[2]

3. Analyse how a large increase in tax on diesel fuel would affect the equilibrium price and quantity of diesel-powered cars. [6]

Answers and quick quiz 6 online ONLINE

Summary

You should have an understanding of:
- what is meant by price
- the relationship between price and worth
- the role of prices in determining an efficient distribution of resources
- what is meant by equilibrium price and quantity
- how to draw the interaction of demand and supply curves
- how to analyse the interaction of demand and supply
- what is meant by the determination of price
- the role of markets in the determination of price
- what is meant by the allocation of resources
- the role of markets in the allocation of resources
- what is meant by market forces
- how the market forces of demand and supply affect equilibrium, price and quantity

OCR GCSE (9-1) Economics

7 Competition

Producers and competition

The key facts about a competitive market are:
- A large number of sellers/producers (see Chapter 1).
- These sellers compete with each other to satisfy the needs and wants of consumers (see Chapter 1).
- Prices are set by the interaction of demand and supply (price mechanism) (see Chapter 6).
- Sellers and buyers, therefore, cannot set either price or quantity in the market.

Competition Where different firms are trying to sell a similar product to a consumer.

Types of competition between producers

REVISED

Price competition	Non-price competition
This means cutting prices	This means any way of competing other than price
Cutting prices leads to more consumer and greater market share	Most obvious is marketing, especially advertising
Those who cannot cut price may go out of business	Offering a specialist service
BUT selling at a price less than the cost of supplying may lead to disaster	Offering a better consumer experience
Price competition is easier for large firms with many products to sell	Offering a better quality product

Typical mistake

Do not think that producers have to make or grow a good. In GCSE Economics a producer can be anyone who sells a good (e.g. a television) or service (e.g. a train ticket) to a consumer.

Exam tip

Remember that competition takes many forms as shown in the table.

Why do producers compete?
- to enter a new market
- to survive in a market
- to make a profit – this will be needed to survive and grow

Now test yourself

TESTED

1 Rooting 4U is a new shop selling fruit and vegetables. The **main** reason it needs to compete as much as possible is to:
   A enter the market
   B make a profit
   C satisfy consumer needs
   D survive in the market

Answers online

How competition affects price

Remember, competition forces price to fall.

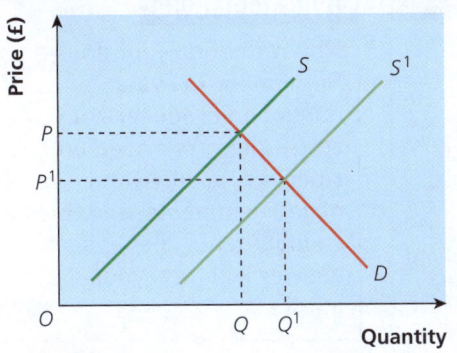

Figure 7.1 Increase in competition

An analysis of the diagram would include the following points:
- Supply curve shifts to the right, S to S^1.
- Price falls, P to P^1.
- Quantity supplied and demanded increases from Q to Q^1.
- The extent of the fall in price and increase in quantity depends on the price elasticity of demand (see Chapter 4 for elasticity of demand):
  - If elastic, fall in price is small and rise in quantity is larger.
  - If inelastic, fall in price is large and rise in quantity is smaller.

Exceptions to the rule that competition leads to a fall in prices would occur due to:
- marketing costs pushing up prices.
- introducing new products can allow firms to charge more at first

The economic impact of competition

Competition is usually assumed to be positive for both consumers and producers. Competition can, however, have negative impacts. Both are shown in the tables below.

Impact of competition on producers

REVISED

If producers do nothing they will lose consumers and face falling profits.

Positive effects	Negative effects
Increase efficiency by:	Lose consumers and possibly go out of business
• cutting costs to maintain profits	May have to replace workers with technology – costs money and workers are often consumers
• innovating to keep supplying consumers with new products	
• improving productivity (see Chapter 8)	

OCR GCSE (9–1) Economics

Impact of competition on consumers

REVISED

Positive effects	Negative effects
Cheaper prices means that consumers can buy more, leading to a rise in living standards	Innovations may be harmful, e.g. use of pesticides on food crops
Improved quality of goods and services	Quality may fall if producers 'cut corners'
Innovation gives consumers more choice	Marketing may persuade consumers to buy what they do not want
Increased consumer sovereignty	

> **Typical mistake**
> Not evaluating your analysis. Remember to evaluate impact on producers or consumers. You need both sides, i.e. positive and negative impacts, and then a judgement – a one-sided answer will limit your marks.

Monopoly and oligopoly

REVISED

- A **monopoly** is a sole producer.
- Legally a monopoly is where one producer has 25% or more of the market.
- **Oligopoly** is a small number of firms controlling the majority of the market.
- Technically, an oligopoly exists if the five largest firms control 50% or more.

> **Monopoly** A sole producer or seller of a good or service.
>
> **Oligopoly** Where a small number of firms control the majority of the market.

How do monopoly and oligopoly differ from competitive markets?

Table 7.1 Differences between monopoly, oligopoly and competitive markets

Difference	Monopoly	Oligopoly	Competitive markets
Size	Usually very large	Can be very large but may also have smaller firms	Normally relatively small
Number of firms	One	A few	Many
Control of prices	Is able to set the price, but cannot then control the quantity	Can influence the price but is restrained by the reaction of rivals. May try to collude	The price is set by the market forces of supply and demand
Level of price and output	In theory, a monopoly will charge a higher price and produce a smaller quantity	Both price and quantity will depend on how strong competitors are and the ability to collude	Price and quantity are both set by market forces. In theory, the price will be lower and the quantity greater
Efficiency	In theory, monopolies are seen as not being efficient, but by achieving large economies of scale they can be efficient	Usually seen as not being economically efficient	Competitive markets normally lead to economic efficiency

Answers and quick quizzes at www.hoddereducation.co.uk/myrevisionnotesdownloads

Exam practice

1. If a firm has a monopoly in a market then:
   A the firm is the only producer
   B the firm will be making a loss
   C there are at least four more large firms
   D there are many buyers and sellers [1]
2. Using an example, explain one method of non-price competition. [2]
3. Evaluate the economic impact of competition on consumers. [6]

Answers and quick quiz 7 online

ONLINE

Summary

You should have an understanding of:
- what is meant by competition between producers in a market economy
- why producers compete
- how to analyse the effects of competition on price
- the effects of competition on producers and consumers
- how to evaluate the effects of this competition
- what is meant by monopoly and oligopoly and how they differ from competitive markets

8 Production

The role of producers, including individuals, firms and the government

The role of producers

Producers:
- may be small, such as an individual, or very large, such as a multinational corporation
- are the supply part of supply and demand
- usually aim to make a **profit**
- employ workers and pay wages (see Chapter 9)

Profit The amount of money a producer has left after all the costs have been paid, i.e. when total revenue is greater than total cost.

Individuals as producers

Type	Examples	Comment
Producers of non-market goods	Cleaning, cooking, childminding	Often only part-time work
Self-employed	Plumbers, joiners, electricians	Work for themselves so keep all the profits

Firms as producers

- May sell to: the local area; the country as a whole; and/or export.
- Small firms are often in a competitive market.
- Large firms may be monopolies or oligopolies (see Chapter 7).
- Larger producers can exercise power over the market (see Chapter 7).

Governments as producers

Type of good or service	Why the government	Private sector
Defence, police etc.	These must be supplied to all or to none	Unwilling to produce as people would not pay
Education, health etc.	Has decided that these need to be available free to everyone	Can supply to those willing to pay
Coal, iron and steel, railways, telecoms etc.	Decided these would be better run in the interest of people by the state	Can provide all and since privatisation has done so

The importance of production and productivity

Production and productivity are not the same. Production is about total output, while productivity is output per unit of input.

> **Production** The total output of goods and services produced by a firm or an industry in a period of time.

Production

REVISED

Production is the total output of goods and services produced by a firm or an industry in a period of time. It involves the use of the factors of production (see Chapter 1).

Advantages of an increase in production	Disadvantages of an increase in production
Increase in employment	Increase may be result of new technology and workers replaced by machines
Rise in standard of living for consumers as more to buy (see Chapter 3)	Workers replaced by machines will have a lower standard of living
Increase in profits	
Can gain larger economies of scale	Average costs may rise leading to diseconomies of scale
Individual firm may gain greater market share	Consequently other firms will lose market share
The country will have economic growth (see Chapter 11)	Could lead to environmental problems

Productivity

REVISED

- **Productivity** is a measure of how efficiently the factors of production are used.
- It is measured as *output per unit of input*.

> **Productivity** The output per unit of input.

How can productivity increase?
- by workers specialising (see Chapter 3)
- through improving the skills of workers by education and training
- through greater investment in new technology
- by increasing the amount of capital equipment

> **Typical mistake**
>
> A common error is to confuse production and productivity. Make sure you are absolutely clear as to their difference.

Why is increased productivity important?

Higher productivity will result in:	Explanation
Lower average costs and increased economies of scale	Firms become more competitive and can compete better both at home and in world markets
Increased profits leading to better training and more investment	Able to attract the best workers. Can pay for research and development of products
Increased total output of the economy	Increases employment and wages: also tax revenue
More export (see Chapters 19, 20 and 22)	Greater economic growth (see Chapter 11)

What are the costs of productivity?

Cost of productivity	Cause of the cost
Unemployment (see Chapter 12) and rise in government expenditure of welfare benefits	Workers replaced by machines and cannot find other employment
Fall in GDP or slower economic growth	Greater international competitiveness leading to retaliation by countries against rising exports

Total cost, average cost, total revenue, average revenue, profit and loss

> **Total cost** All the costs of the firm added together.
>
> **Average cost** The cost of producing a unit of output (unit cost of production).

Although these are six different concepts, do note the links between them. This will help with both the explanations and the calculations.

Total cost

REVISED

Total cost consists of fixed costs such as marketing, and variable costs such as raw materials.

Total cost (TC) = total fixed cost (TFC) + total variable cost (TVC)

Average cost

REVISED

Average cost is the cost of producing a unit of output. A fall in average cost leads to economies of scale and shows the firm is becoming more efficient.

$$\text{Average cost (AC)} = \frac{\text{total cost (TC)}}{\text{quantity (Q)}}$$

Now test yourself

TESTED

1 Complete the table by calculating TC and AC.

Output	Total fixed cost (£)	Total variable cost (£)	Total cost (£)	Average cost (£)
5	50	30		
10	50	50		
15	50	70		
20	50	90		

Answers online

Total revenue

REVISED

Total revenue is the total income of a firm from the sale of its goods and services.

Total revenue (TR) = price of the product (P) × quantity sold (Q)

> **Total revenue** The total income of the firm from the sale of its goods and services.

Average revenue

REVISED

Average revenue is the revenue per unit sold and is equal to the price.

$$\text{Average revenue (AR)} = \frac{\text{total revenue (TR)}}{\text{quantity (Q)}}$$

> **Average revenue** The revenue per unit sold.

Now test yourself

TESTED

2 Complete the table by calculating TR and AR.

Price (£)	Quantity	Total revenue (£)	Average revenue (£)
10	50		
8	100		
6	150		

Answers online

Profit and loss

REVISED

Profit is when a firm gains more revenue than it pays out in costs. TR > TC.

Loss is where a firm's revenue is less than its costs. TR < TC.

Profit/Loss = total revenue (TR) − total cost (TC)

> **Profit** The amount of money a seller has left after all the costs have been paid.
>
> **Loss** When a firm's revenue is less than its costs.

> **Exam tip**
>
> Make sure you know how to calculate all these terms. Remember to show the money sign (£) and that a loss is negative (−).

The importance of cost, revenue, profit and loss for producers

Cost

REVISED

- Costs rise as output increases leading to an upward sloping supply curve (see Chapter 5).
- Firms control costs to try to make a (bigger) profit.
- If costs fall firms can supply more at every price (see Chapter 5).

Revenue

REVISED

- Without sufficient revenue a firm will make a loss and go out of business.
- Revenue growth, leading to greater profit, encourages investment in the firm leading to expansion.
- A steady level of revenue allows firms to gain loans and favourable interest rate on overdrafts.
- Creates confidence in the firm: workers remain and suppliers will supply more.

Profit

REVISED

- Acts as a signal to resources to move to the firm.
- Provides money for investment.
- Offers a measure of the success of investments and encourages more in the future.

Loss

REVISED

- A continuous loss will result in a firm closing down.
- In the short run, however, a loss can be covered by using money previously saved or by loans.
- Acts as a signal to resources to move away from the firm.

Economies of scale

Economies of scale is where an increase in the scale of production results in a fall in the average costs of production. Internal economies refer to the growth of the firm itself. External economies are benefits from belonging to an industry (all firms gain) or its location.

Economies of scale The cost advantages a firm can gain by increasing the scale of production.

Type of internal economy of scale	Explanation
Division of labour	Dividing work up into small specialist areas to increase speed
Financial	Larger firms can borrow money at lower interest rates
Increased dimensions	Size (volume) increases faster than costs
Managerial	Larger firms can employ more specialists: increase efficiency
Marketing	Larger firms can promote more products with their budget
Purchasing or bulk-buying	Buying large quantities at a time leads to discounts
Risk-bearing	Large firms offer a wide range of products in case one fails
Research and development	Larger firms can afford to have their own R&D department
Technical	Larger firms can afford more and better capital equipment

Typical mistake

A very common error is to state that economies of scale only apply to large firms. Firms of *all sizes* can achieve economies of scale.

Type of external economy of scale	Explanation
Concentration of firms	Suppliers of parts may locate near the main producer
Education and training facilities	Local university may run courses to suit the needs of firms
Location	An area with a good reputation may attract more firms
Transport	Better transport links will help reduce costs

Exam practice

1. Which of the following would be most likely to increase productivity of workers?
   A a rise in the standard of living
   B an increase in the profits of firms
   C greater emphasis on training courses
   D larger economies of scale [1]
2. Explain one way in which an individual can act as a producer. [2]
3. Evaluate the statement that 'it is important for producers to make a profit and to always avoid making a loss'. [6]

Answers and quick quiz 8 online

ONLINE

Summary

You should have an understanding of:
- the role of producers including individuals, firms and government
- what is meant by production and productivity and the differences between them
- how to evaluate the importance of production and productivity for the economy
- what is meant by total cost, average cost, total revenue, average revenue, profit and loss
- how to calculate total cost, average cost, total revenue, average revenue, profit and loss
- how to evaluate the importance of cost, revenue, profit and loss for producers, including how costs and revenues affect profit and supply
- what is meant by economies of scale
- the different types of internal economies of scale
- the different types of external economies of scale

9 The labour market

The role and operation of the labour market

The **labour market** consists of the supply of labour by households and the demand for labour by firms. In addition to supply and demand, the price of labour (wages) is influenced by governments and trade unions.

> **Labour market** Where workers sell their labour and employers buy the labour.

The role of the labour market

REVISED

The role of the labour market is to:
- enable workers who are willing and able to sell their labour to meet employers who are willing and able to offer them a job
- determine the wage rate or salary for this work

The operation of the labour market

REVISED

- The labour market operates on a local, national (UK) and international basis.
- Some jobs require specific qualifications or skills, while others are geographically fixed.
- The labour market depends on the exchange of information between employers and employees on: wage rates, employment conditions, level of competition, location etc.
- It lacks perfect mobility, i.e. workers cannot move to any job that is available.

Reason for lack of labour mobility	Explanation
Lack of necessary skills	Skills needed in different jobs are not interchangeable
Unable/unwilling to relocate	Speaking only English – restricted to jobs in English-speaking countries
Personal factors	Family ties to an area or would prefer to live in certain areas
Information failure (see Chapter 18)	Not aware of what jobs are available

Interaction between workers and employers

REVISED

Figure 9.1 The interaction of workers and employers

The interaction shown applies to any aspect of work such as the number of hours.

Type of interaction	Explanation
Individual worker and employer	The worker deals directly with employer about pay etc.
Collective bargaining	Trade unions bargain for all their members with employer

NB The interaction will take place within a legal framework set by the government, such as health and safety regulations.

The determination of wages through supply and demand

If you are not sure how supply and demand determine price, go back to Chapter 6.

Remember that wages can be determined by other factors such as discrimination and government intervention.

The determination of wages through supply and demand

REVISED

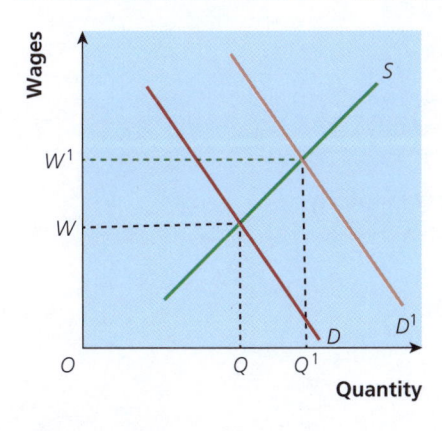

Figure 9.2 The effect of an increase in the demand for labour

OCR GCSE (9-1) Economics 53

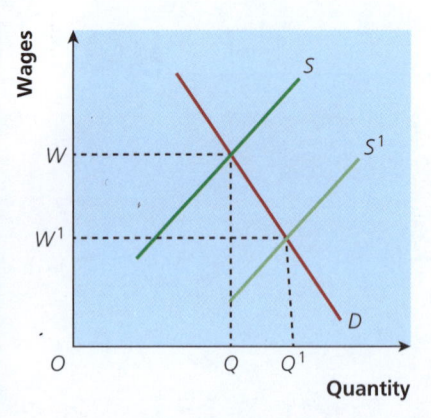

Figure 9.3 The effect of an increase in the supply of labour

- If demand for labour increases (see below for possible causes), then the demand curve moves from D to D^1. This leads to an increase in wages from W to W^1 and an increase in the supply and demand for labour from Q to Q^1.
- Similarly, if supply of labour increases (see below for possible causes), then the supply curve moves from S to S^1. This leads to a fall in wages from W to W^1 *but* an increase in the supply and demand for labour from Q to Q^1.

> **Exam tip**
>
> Remember to use *W* for wages and not *P* for price when drawing labour market diagrams.

How price elasticity affects the determination of wages

If you are not sure about price elasticity go back to Chapters 4 for demand and 5 for supply.

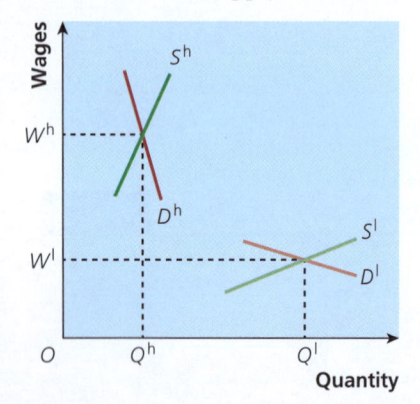

Figure 9.4 Market for CEOs and shop assistants

Figure 9.5 Wages when supply is totally inelastic

The size of the change in both wage and quantity will depend on the PED of, and PES for, labour.

- If PED and PES are both inelastic, shown by D^h and S^h in the figure, then the wage may be high as employers are willing to pay a high price to get the right person/people and the supply is limited.
- If PED and PES are both elastic, shown by D^l and S^l in the figure, then the wage may be low as employers do not want as many people if wages rise and the supply is plentiful.
- Where PES is totally inelastic, unique talent, then the wage is totally dependent on how many want to employ the person, as shown by the shift in demand from D to D^1.

Answers and quick quizzes at www.hoddereducation.co.uk/myrevisionnotesdownloads

Now test yourself

TESTED

Draw diagrams to show:
1 A fall in demand for labour, where PES is a) elastic, and b) inelastic.

   a)

   b)

2 A fall in supply for labour where PED is a) elastic, and b) inelastic.

   a)

   b)

For each, write a brief analysis.

Answers online

Factors affecting the supply and demand of labour

REVISED

- Demand for labour depends on the demand for the product that labour helps to produce/sell.
- Supply of labour is those who are willing and able to work. This consists of those in work and those who are seeking work, including the unemployed (working population).
- A rise in wages, however, may result in more people who are currently inactive, such as those who are ill, looking after the family, discouraged or retired, being willing to work.

Factors affecting the demand for labour

Factors	Explanation
Demand for products	If demand for a product increases then more labour is demanded
Wage rates	The demand for labour has an inverse relationship with wages
Real wages	If real wages fall then labour may replace capital
Productivity of labour	If labour productivity rises then higher wages can be paid
Profits of firms	If profits increase then firms expand and take on more labour
State of the economy	A growing economy is likely to require more labour

Factors affecting the supply of labour

Factors	Explanation
Wage rate	The higher the wage the more people are willing to work
Other monetary payments	Higher pay through overtime/productivity pay will increase supply
Non-monetary factors	Better working conditions/promotion chances will increase supply
Education and training	Will increase the supply of skilled labour
Barriers to entry	Qualifications/trade unions/discrimination may reduce supply
Size of working population	More migrants/increased retirement age etc. will increase supply

Gross and net pay

- **Gross pay** is the actual amount your employer has paid you before deductions.
- **Net pay** is the amount you 'take home' after deductions: Net pay = gross pay − deductions.
- Deductions consist of **income tax**, **national insurance** and **pension** contributions.
- Both national insurance and pensions contributions require both the worker and the employer to pay.

> **Gross pay** The amount of money that an employee earns before any deductions are made.
>
> **Net pay** The amount of money that an employee is left with after deductions are made from gross pay.
>
> **Income tax** A tax levied on personal income, i.e. a tax on a person's wages.
>
> **National insurance** A contribution paid by workers and their employers towards the cost of state benefits.
>
> **Pension** A fixed amount paid at regular intervals to a person (usually retired) or their surviving dependents.

Calculating gross and net pay

REVISED

Table 9.1 Calculation of gross pay

Payment per month	£
Wage	2,000
Bonus	200
Total	2,200

To calculate gross pay:
- Start with base pay — the amount your contract states you are paid.
- If this is so much per hour then multiply the hours by the amount per hour: W × hours.
- Add on extra payments such as bonuses or overtime.

Table 9.2 Calculation of net pay

Gross pay and deductions per annum	£
Gross pay	24,000
Income tax	2,512
National insurance	1,925
Pension contribution	1,440
Net pay	18,123

To calculate net pay, as in net pay table:
- Start with gross pay.
- Take away the deductions: income tax, national insurance and pension contribution.

Exam practice

1 Which of the following is a factor affecting the supply of labour?
   A existence of a local labour market
   B size of the working population
   C the productivity of labour
   D the profitability of the firms in the market [1]
2 Marie earned £34,000 last year. She paid £4,800 in income tax, £3,069 in national insurance and £6,059 into her pension.
   Calculate Marie's net pay last year. Show your workings. [2]
3 Analyse how an increase in the demand for British made electric cars could affect the demand for labour. [6]

Answers and quick quiz 9 online

Summary

You should have an understanding of:
- what is meant by the labour market
- the role of the labour market and how it operates
- what is meant by the interaction of workers and employers
- how to analyse the determination of wages through supply and demand
- how price elasticity affects the determination of wages
- the factors affecting the demand for labour
- the factors affecting the supply of labour
- what is meant by gross and net pay
- what the deductions from gross pay are
- how to calculate gross and net pay

10 The role of money and financial markets

The role of money as a medium of exchange

Money consists of notes, coins and bank deposits. Cheques, debit and credit cards and various forms of electronic payments are not money.

The role of money

REVISED

- **Money** is anything that is generally acceptable as a means of payment for goods and services.
- Money avoids the need for barter.

The following are money	The following are not money
Bank notes	Debit cards
Coins	Credit cards
Savings accounts	Cheques
Current accounts	

> **Money** Anything that is acceptable as a means of payment for goods and services.
>
> **Medium of exchange** Anything that sets the standard of value of goods and services acceptable to all parties involved in a transaction.

Medium of exchange

REVISED

- **Medium of exchange** is anything that enables people to engage in the exchange of goods and services without having to barter.
- As money is widely accepted for the buying and selling of products it acts as a medium of exchange.

> **Now test yourself** TESTED
>
> 1 If you went into a shop to buy a new pair of trousers and paid £30, explain how this shows that money is a medium of exchange.
>
> Answers online

The role of the financial sector

The **financial sector** consists of financial organisations and their products, and involves the flow of capital (see Chapter 1).

> **Financial sector** Consists of financial organisations and their products and involves the flow of capital.

The role of the financial sector for the economy

REVISED

- The finanical sector helps consumers, firms and governments to carry out economic activities.
- It, therefore, helps the market to work.

58 Answers and quick quizzes at www.hoddereducation.co.uk/myrevisionnotesdownloads

- It involves the lending and borrowing of money through, for example, **banks** and **building societies**.
- Banks and building societies enable people who do not need to use money now, savers, to provide it for those who need it now, borrowers.
- This allows for supply of money, from savers, to equal demand for money, from borrowers.

> **Banks** Financial institutions licensed to receive deposits and make loans.
>
> **Building societies** Mutual financial organisations that are owned by their members.

The role of banks

REVISED

- Banks are financial institutions licensed to receive deposits and make loans.
- They may also provide financial services, such as wealth management, currency exchange and safe deposit boxes.
- There are two types of banks: commercial/retail banks and investment banks. In most countries, banks are regulated by the national government or central bank (in the UK, the Bank of England).
- Examples of commercial banks include: Barclays; HSBC; Lloyds; Metro; Royal Bank of Scotland; Santander.

Central banks and commercial banks

Central banks	Commercial banks
Issue bank notes: supervise the supply of money	Accept deposits (savings) and pay interest
Control monetary policy (see Chapter 16): sets the bank rate which determines all other interest rates	Make payments for customers by mobile phone/card payments or bank transfers
Provides financial stability	Make payments by accepting cheques
Manages the country's foreign reserves	Issue loans to individuals and firms
Acts as the bank for the commercial banks	Provide foreign currencies for firms and individuals
Acts as the bank for the government	Offer safe deposit boxes

Investment banks

Examples include: Goldman Sachs; Morgan Stanley; Rothschilds; UBS.

These help firms with specialist needs:
- in mergers and takeovers.
- underwriting share issues (guaranteeing all will be sold)
- with international trade including financial conditions in new markets

The role of building societies

REVISED

Examples include: Coventry; Cumberland; Nationwide; Nottingham; Skipton.

OCR GCSE (9-1) Economics 59

The people who save money with them are their members. The differences between banks and building societies are:

Building societies	Banks
Mutual organisations	Public limited companies (PLCs)
Owned by members who are savers with them	Owned by shareholders
Provide a limited range of services mainly savings and mortgages (loans for houses)	Wide range of services (see above)
Limited as to how much money can be borrowed from the money market	Can borrow widely on the money market

The role of insurance companies

REVISED

Insurance companies are financial institutions that guarantee compensation for specified loss, damage, illness or death in return for payments. They pools clients' risks to make payments more affordable for the insured. Examples include: Aviva; Legal & General; LV=; Prudential; Zurich.

Insurance Is a contract, represented by a policy, in which an individual or organisation receives financial protection, or reimbursement against losses, from an insurance company.

Function	Explanation
Life insurance	Pays out money to the surviving family. Intended to help replace the loss of income due to death
	Also: long-term savings, pensions and annuities for retirement
General insurance	All non-life aspects: property; contents; motor; health; pets etc.

The importance of the financial sector

Role	Consumers	Producers	Government
Credit provision	Can buy now, pay later and thus increase consumption	Can borrow money to expand	Can run a budget deficit (see Chapter 15) or spend before taxes are collected
Liquidity provision	Can borrow to pay later – often against an asset like a house	Banks will provide overdraft facilities so firms can continue trading while waiting for payments	
Risk management	Allow savers to spread their risk by putting their money into a range of companies, rather than just one	Reduces risk of not receiving payment, especially when exporting, or not receiving on time	Allows for vital expenditure even when revenue is uncertain

The 2008 financial crises was caused by the financial sector creating too much liquidity and credit while lending money beyond the means of borrowers to repay.

How different interest rates affect the levels of saving, borrowing and investment

Different interest rates do not mean just higher or lower, but that there are many different interest rates in the financial market.

How different interest rates affect the levels of saving

REVISED

Saving is mainly done by individuals.

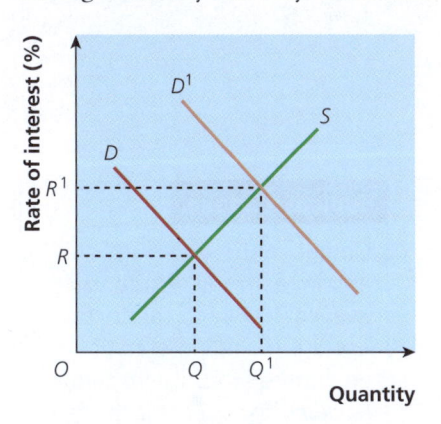

Figure 10.1 The effect of a change in the rate of interest on savings

- The opportunity cost (see Chapter 2) of spending is the loss of interest payable on savings.
- As the rate of interest rises, R to R^1, people tend to save more, Q to Q^1.
- As the rate of interest falls, R^1 to R, people tend to save less, Q^1 to Q.

How interest rates affect the levels of borrowing

REVISED

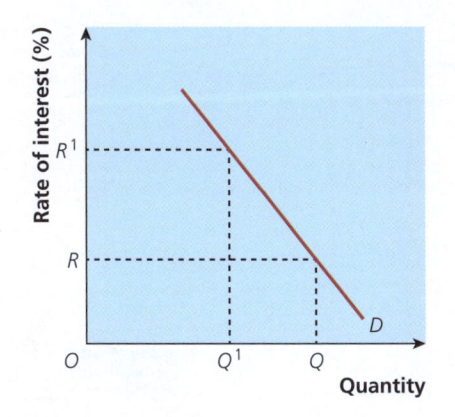

Figure 10.2 Demand for money

> **Exam tip**
> When the exam question asks you to *analyse*, you should demonstrate the ability to present logical chains of reasoning based on knowledge and application. It involves the use of economic terms and the explanation of diagrams.

> **Saving** Is the part of an individual's income which is not spent on consumption.
>
> **Borrowing** Is receiving money (or something of value) in exchange for an obligation to pay it back at a specified time in the future.
>
> **Investment** Is the purchase of capital goods that are used to produce future goods and services. It is also an asset purchased to provide income in the future and/or to be sold for profit.

OCR GCSE (9–1) Economics 61

The analysis below refers to a rise in interest rates. The reverse will be true for a fall.
- A rise in the rate of interest, R to R^1, will lead to an increase in the cost of borrowing.
- This rise leads to consumers and producers borrowing less, Q to Q^1, and maybe to save more.
- A rise in interest rates is likely to lead to exports costing more (see Chapter 21) so producers sell less, receive less revenue and are less likely to expand or need as much money.

How interest rates affect the levels of investment

REVISED

Investment is mainly done by producers and governments.

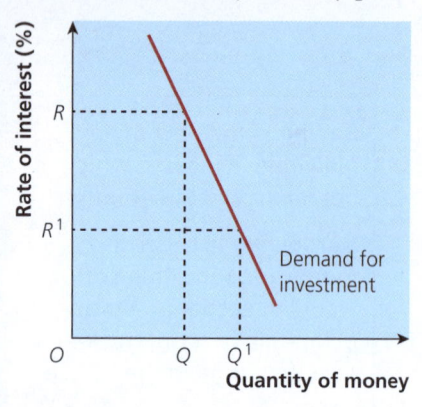

Figure 10.3 Level of investment inversely related to the rate of interest

> **Typical mistake**
>
> Do not confuse saving and investment. While in everyday speech the terms are often used in place of each other, *in Economics they have precise meanings* – see definitions on page 61.

- Level of investment is inversely related to the rate of interest.
- As rate of interest falls, R to R^1, the level of investment increases, Q to Q^1.
- Lower interest rates encourage consumption so firms need to expand and thus invest.

If consumers lack confidence in the economy then demand may not increase so investment will not increase as interest rates fall.

The effect on savings and borrowings of changes in the rate of interest

We have explained how the rate of interest affects savings and borrowings. In this section we show how these effects can be calculated.

The effect on savings

REVISED

Mark has savings of £5,000 on deposit at 2% rate of interest.

He receives £5,000 × $\frac{2}{100}$ = £100.

If the rate of interest rises to 3%, he receives £5,000 × $\frac{3}{100}$ = £150.

The effect on borrowings

REVISED

Eileen wants to borrow £100,000 to buy a house. The rate of interest is 7%.

The interest she will pay is £100,000 × $\frac{7}{100}$ = £7,000.

If the rate of interest falls to 6%, then she will pay £100,000 × $\frac{6}{100}$ = £6,000.

Exam practice

1 Which of the following defines money?
   A anything that is acceptable as a form of payment
   B consists of notes, coins and bank deposits
   C is a means of buying a good or service and paying later
   D is the standard of value of goods and services [1]
2 Calculate the effect of a change in the rate of interest from 4% to 3.5% on a saver who has £8,000 on deposit in a bank. Show your workings. [2]
3 Evaluate the importance of the financial sector for producers. [6]

Answers and quick quiz 10 online

ONLINE

Summary

You should have an understanding of:
- what is meant by money
- what is meant by medium of exchange
- the role of the financial sector in the economy
- the role of banks, building societies and insurance companies
- how to evaluate the importance of the financial sector for consumers, producers and governments
- what is meant by savings, investment and borrowing
- how to analyse how interest rates affect savings, borrowing and investment
- how to calculate the effect on savings and borrowing of changes in the rate of interest

11 Economic growth

Meaning of economic growth

- **Economic growth** is an increase in the economic activity in a country.
- This is shown by the growth in the value of output.
- The total value of output is called **gross domestic product (GDP)**.
- The total value of output produced is equal to the total of incomes in an economy.
- It is also equal to the total spent in an economy.
- For example, if a student purchased a textbook for £20, the bookseller's output would be £20, their income from the sale would be £20, and the student would have spent £20.
- So when there is economic growth, output, incomes and spending are rising.

Economic growth Increase in GDP over time.

Gross domestic product (GDP) The value of output produced within a country in a year.

Total output = Total income = Total spending

Figure 11.1 Economic activity in an economy

Measurement of economic growth

- To calculate economic growth, the government measures the value of output and calculates the rate at which it has changed.
- It is measured by the percentage change in GDP.
- The formula to calculate economic growth is:

$$\frac{\text{change in GDP}}{\text{original GDP}} \times 100$$

- For instance, if GDP in 2019 is £800bn and in 2020 is £880bn, the increase in GDP is £80bn and economic growth is 10%.
- Total GDP figures are useful to show the size of an economy as a whole.
- Total GDP is calculated by adding together the value of all output of goods and services in an economy.

Exam tip

Check whether a question is asking for a change in output or a percentage change

Now test yourself

1. GDP in Country A was US$250 billion in 2017 and US$300 billion in 2018. Calculate the economic growth.
2. GDP in country B was £100,000,000 in 2017 and £98,000,000 in 2018. Calculate the economic growth.
3. GDP in Country C was £400 billion in 2017 and economic growth was 5%. Calculate the level of GDP in 2018.

Answers online

GDP per capita

- **GDP per capita** is calculated by dividing total GDP by population size.
- This gives output per person, which is also average income per person.
- GDP per capita is a useful figure to compare between countries and over time as population sizes vary.
- It can be used to measure the standard of living in a country, as it shows how much income people have to buy goods and services.
- However, incomes may not be spread evenly within an economy.

> **GDP per capita** GDP divided by population.

Recent and historical data

- Figure 11.2 shows the UK's annual rate of growth over a 10-year period (i.e. the percentage change in GDP).
- If economic growth is positive and high over a period of time, it is called a boom.
- If economic growth is negative over a period of time, it is called a recession.
- Technically, economists say that a recession is when GDP falls for two or more consecutive quarters (i.e. 6 months).

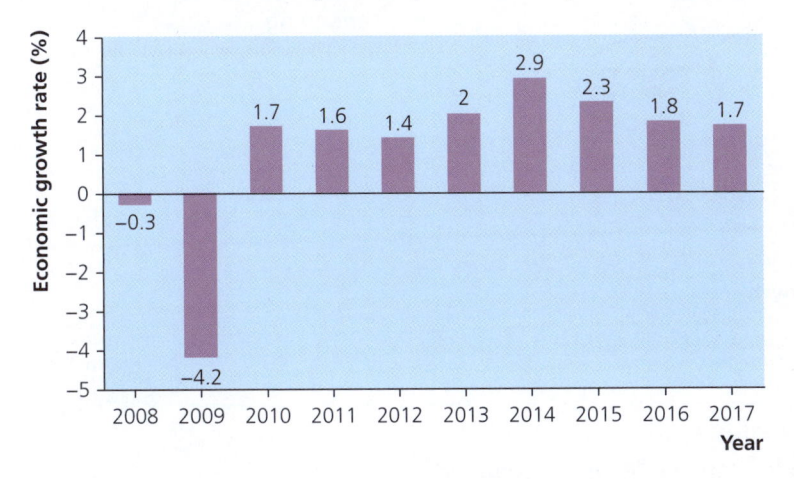

Figure 11.2 UK annual economic growth rates, 2008–17

Source: www.ons.gov.uk

- During 2008 the UK went into recession.
- Output fell in the UK – as shown by the negative numbers.
- One likely impact of recession is that fewer workers are needed to produce the lower level of output.
- This may lead to an increase in unemployment and a decrease in incomes.
- This may also lead to a fall in spending which leads to fewer goods and services being demanded.
- In turn this leads to a fall in output and the cycle continues.
- This may be partly why the recession continued into 2009.
- Between 2010 and 2017 there was a positive annual growth rate, which shows that output was rising again.

Determinants of economic growth

- Economic growth can be caused by an increased ability of an economy to supply goods and services.
- The quality or quantity of factors of production affect an economy's potential to make goods and services.
- Determinants of economic growth change the quality or quantity of these factors of production.

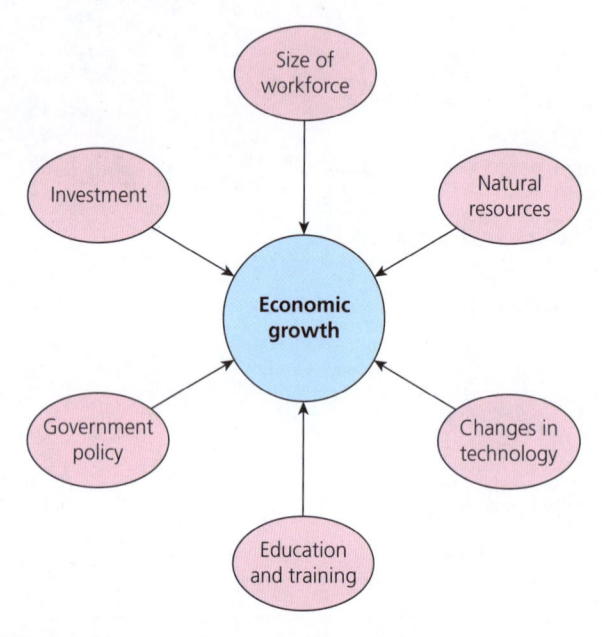

Exam tip

To analyse these determinants of economic growth, you need to be able to explain how they might cause economic growth using logical chains of reasoning.

Figure 11.3 Determinants of economic growth

Investment

REVISED

Investment is spending on capital goods by firms.
- Capital goods are man-made aids to production, e.g. delivery vehicles and computers.
- They can be faster or more efficient than workers doing a job.
- They might also be used by workers to help them work more efficiently.
- This can lead to the economy being able to make more in the future.

Changes in technology

REVISED

- Advances in technology can improve the quality of capital goods.
- This means the same amount of capital can make more goods and services.
- For instance, if a restaurant's oven is replaced with a newer oven that heats up faster, then the restaurant can now serve customers more quickly and their output could increase.
- Improved capital may mean a country can use all its other factors of production more efficiently.

Size of workforce

REVISED

- The size of workforce, or labour force, is the quantity of people who are willing and able to work in an economy.
- This is the number of people who either have jobs or are looking for them.
- An increase in the number of potential workers in a country can mean that more can be made.
- This is because there is an increase in the factors of production.
- For instance, an increase in immigration may increase the quantity of labour available to work.

Education and training

REVISED

- Education and training can affect the quality, and quantity, of the labour factor of production.
- An increase in spending on education may lead to more skilled workers in the future.
- These workers are more productive and can increase how many goods and services they make.
- This increase in output could mean an increase in GDP and economic growth.

Natural resources

REVISED

- The quantity of natural resources available affects the land factor of production.
- If a country finds new natural resources, e.g. oil, it can either sell them to other countries or use them to make more goods and services.
- Both of these could lead to an increase in output, GDP and economic growth.
- A country may also face a decrease in its natural resources, such as losing land due to rising sea levels.
- This can mean it is less able to make as much output and economic growth may decrease or become negative.

Government policies

REVISED

- The amount of government intervention in a country will depend on the type of economy: command, mixed or market.
- A government may have policies that affect specific markets or ones that impact the whole economy.
- One example of intervention that might help the supply side of an economy is for the government to spend money on providing infrastructure, such as roads and broadband.
- Improved infrastructure can make it easier for producers to supply goods and services, by increasing their efficiency and reducing their costs.
- This can lead to an increase in output, GDP and economic growth.
- Government policies can also affect total demand within an economy and economic growth, e.g. income tax levels.

Exam tip

To work out whether there is a positive or negative impact on supply and potential economic growth, think about whether the intervention makes it easier/harder or more costly/cheaper to produce.

Costs and benefits of economic growth

Benefits of economic growth

REVISED

- Economic growth means an economy can make more output.
- This may be beneficial as there could be a greater supply of goods and services available to buy, which may lead to a decrease in prices and an increase in living standards of consumers.
- More workers may be needed to make the extra output, which leads to more jobs and less unemployment.
- The government may receive more tax revenue (e.g. through increased income tax due to more people working), which can be used to improve the welfare of society (e.g. by improving healthcare).
- An increase in tax revenue combined with falling government spending on unemployment benefits may improve the budget balance.

Costs of economic growth

REVISED

- Pollution and quality of life: more production may create more pollution, harming health.
- Pollution and the environment: increased production may harm the environment, e.g. water pollution kills fish, which has a negative impact on fishermen.
- Congestion: if output increases, more inputs and goods have to be transported around the country.
- Depletion of resources: more raw materials are needed to make more output, so non-renewable resources are used up and the ability to produce in the future is reduced.
- Workplace stress: increased output might be achieved by increased pressure on workers, which can impact mental health.
- Inflation: if demand rises faster than supply, there is more competition between consumers for goods and price levels rise.
- International competitiveness: inflation makes a country's goods seem relatively more expensive than those from other countries and can result in a drop in demand.
- Inequality: economic growth leads to increased average incomes, but there could be increased inequality if the increase in incomes is not evenly spread between people.

> **Exam tip**
>
> Consider a specific type of pollution to make chains of reasoning clearer when explaining an environmental cost of economic growth.

Economic, social and environmental sustainability

- Economic growth should improve the quality of life now without reducing it for future generations.
- The costs or benefits of economic growth can have an impact on factors of production both now and into the future.

- Increased production due to more output during economic growth may lead to more air pollution that may cause global warming which could harm economic stability:
  - through reduced factors of production, such as land due to rising sea levels, reducing future production, e.g. of crops
  - if it leads to people's homes being lost in flooding due to rising sea levels, which would reduce quality of life for many people in the future
  - many areas of the world may experience more extreme weather so the countryside is damaged in the future

Exam practice

1. State two determinants of economic growth. [2]
2. Using Table 11.1, calculate the total GDP in the UK in 2008. Show your workings. [2]

Table 11.1 Gross domestic product of the UK (quarterly estimates)

Time period (quarters of a year)	GDP value (in millions)
2007 Q4	£455,043
2008 Q1	£456,663
2008 Q2	£453,283
2008 Q3	£445,818
2008 Q4	£436,137
2009 Q1	£428,886

Source: www.ons.gov.uk

3. Using Table 11.1, calculate the average quarterly GDP of the UK in 2008. Round to two decimal places. Show your workings. [2]
4. Using Table 11.1, calculate the percentage change in GDP between Q3 and Q4 of 2008. [2]
5. Using the information in Table 11.1, explain what happened to the value of GDP between 2007 Q4 and 2008 Q1. [2]

   Note: in a real paper there would not be so many similar questions together
6. Analyse how determinants of economic growth can lead to an increase in output in an economy. [6]

Answers and quick quiz 11 online

ONLINE

Summary

You should have an understanding of:
- the meaning of economic growth
- how to calculate economic growth
- the measurements of economic growth using GDP and GDP per capita
- how to analyse recent and historical GDP data
- how to analyse the determinants of economic growth: investment, technology, workforce, education and training, natural resources and government policies
- how to evaluate the costs and benefits of economic growth
- how to evaluate the impact of economic growth on economic, social and environmental sustainability

12 Low unemployment

Employment and unemployment

Employment

REVISED

- **Employment** means people have a job, e.g. work for a firm or are self-employed.
- People who are willing and able to work make up the labour force or workforce.
- The labour factor of production is used, or employed, to make goods and services.
- Wages incentivise and motivate people to work.
- Full employment is when everyone willing to work is able to get a job.
- There will not be 100% employment in a country as there will always be some people moving between jobs.
- As demand and supply change for goods and services, so will the need for workers within these different markets, so there will always be some people looking for new jobs.

Employment When people who are willing and able to work can find a job. (It also refers to the use of labour in a country to produce goods and services.)

Unemployment When people who are willing and able to work cannot find a job.

Unemployment

REVISED

- **Unemployment** means that people who are of working age and are looking for work at the current wage rate are unable to find a job.
- The working age usually includes people above 16 years old.
- People who are economically inactive are not included in the workforce or unemployment figures.
- Economically inactive includes pensioners, full-time students, those who are sick or looking after family full-time.
- A key government objective is to achieve low unemployment because people then receive wages.
- Wages are a main source of income and can help people out of poverty.
- Low unemployment means less money is needed by the government for unemployment benefits.

The Claimant Count

- A method of measuring unemployment is the **Claimant Count**.
- The Claimant Count includes people who are claiming unemployment-related benefits.
- These include the Jobseeker's Allowance (JSA) and universal credit (UC).
- Benefits are a way for those without jobs to get money to pay for essential goods and services.
- The need to claim these benefits in order to have a basic standard of living should mean that the unemployed are likely to register for them.
- This makes it a method the UK government can use to estimate the **level of unemployment**.

Claimant Count A measurement of unemployment using the number of people who claim unemployment-related benefits.

Level of unemployment The total number of people who are in the workforce and are without a job.

Calculation of unemployment rate

- The unemployment rate is the percentage of the country's workforce that is unemployed.
- It can be calculated as follows:

$$\text{Unemployment rate} = \frac{\text{number of unemployed}}{\text{workforce}} \times 100$$

- The level of unemployment and unemployment rate can move in different directions.
- For instance, the level of unemployment can increase in a country, but if the size of the workforce increases by proportionally more, then the unemployment rate falls.
- A rising unemployment rate over time can mean economic growth is slowing down or has become negative, so fewer workers are needed to produce less output.
- A falling unemployment rate over time can mean there is economic growth so more workers are needed to produce more output.

> **Exam tip**
>
> If a question is about the level of unemployment, the answer should be a number along with the correct unit of measurement, such as millions. If a question is about the rate of unemployment, the answer should be a percentage.

Now test yourself

1. In 2018, country A has a workforce of 6 million people and 450,000 people unemployed. Calculate the unemployment rate.
2. The number of people unemployed in country A increases by 2019 by 6%. Calculate the number of people now unemployed.
3. The workforce in country A also increases by 10% in 2019. Calculate the new unemployment rate (to two decimal places).

Answers online

Recent and historical data

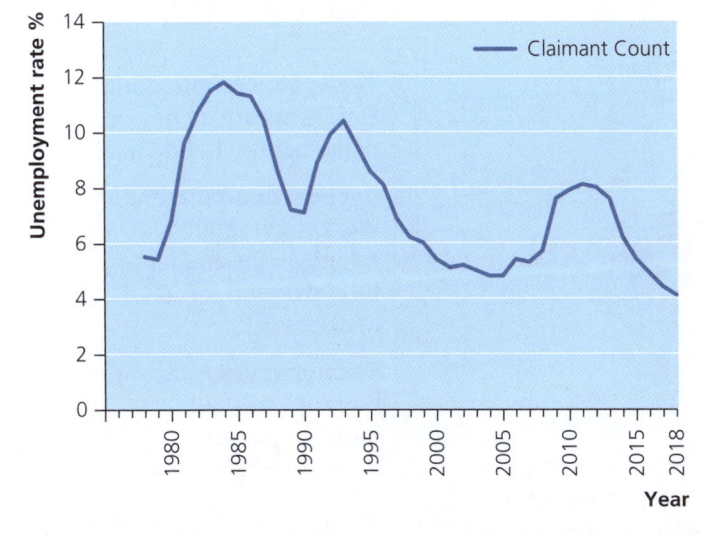

Figure 12.1 UK unemployment rates, 1978–2018

Source: www.ons.gov.uk

- Over time in the UK, the unemployment rate has both risen and fallen.
- Figure 12.1 was produced by the Office for National Statistics using data from the Labour Force Survey.
- It shows a similar pattern to the figures that could have been plotted using the Claimant Count.
- The unemployment rate rose at points in the 1980s, 1990s and from 2007 to 2011.
- This often linked to problems in the economy where output fell and fewer workers were needed to make this lower level of goods and services.
- Since 2011 the unemployment rate in the UK has fallen.
- Some of these new jobs have been in low-paid, low-skilled areas, e.g. warehouse staff.
- Employing workers may be a cheaper alternative, compared to the cost of buying machinery.
- There has been an increase in self-employment, e.g. Uber drivers, which reduces risks and costs for firms but leaves individuals with fewer employment rights.

Causes and types of unemployment

- Unemployment may be affected by, or worsened by, a range of different causes.
- These are referred to as types of unemployment.
- These may vary between individuals and different regions of the country.
- If a government identifies the causes of unemployment, it can change its policies.

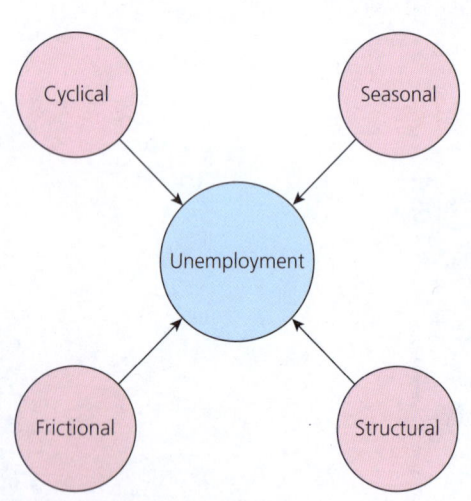

Figure 12.2 Types of unemployment

- There are four key **types of unemployment**:
  - **Cyclical unemployment**: caused by problems in the economy, so total demand falls and fewer workers are needed to make less output.
  - **Frictional unemployment**: caused when people are 'between jobs' for a short time, i.e. someone has left a job and is due to start a new job soon.
  - **Seasonal unemployment**: caused when labour is only demanded at certain times of year, e.g. fewer ice cream sellers are needed in the winter in the UK as there is less demand for ice cream.
  - **Structural unemployment**: caused due to changes in demand and supply. Certain industries decline and jobs in these areas are reduced, e.g. steel production in the UK.

Types of unemployment
Different causes of workers being unable to find a job.

Cyclical unemployment
Workers without employment due to a fall in total demand for goods and services.

Frictional unemployment
Workers without employment as they move from one job to another.

Seasonal unemployment
Workers without employment due to a decrease in demand at certain times of year.

Structural unemployment
Workers without employment due to the decline of an industry.

> **Now test yourself** — TESTED
>
> 4 Match the terms with the correct explanation.
>
> | 1 | Employment | A | Workers without employment moving from one job to another |
> | 2 | Frictional unemployment | B | Different causes of workers being unable to find a job |
> | 3 | Structural unemployment | C | This is when people who are willing and able to work cannot find a job |
> | 4 | Types of unemployment | D | Workers without employment due to the decline of an industry |
> | 5 | Unemployment | E | This is when people who are willing and able to work can find a job |
>
> Answers online

Consequences of unemployment

Benefits of unemployment — REVISED

- Easier to recruit: if there are more workers looking for employment, it is easier for firms to find new workers and expand output.
- Dynamic economy: unemployed workers help an economy to be responsive if they can move from one industry to another as demand patterns change.
- International competitiveness: workers may have to accept a lower wage rate to get a job, which reduces costs for firms, meaning they can lower prices and be more price competitive against overseas firms
- Inflation: lower wages mean individuals can afford to buy less, so there is less demand for goods, resulting in lower general price level.

Costs of unemployment — REVISED

For individuals:
- Lower standard of living: individuals have less income, so can afford fewer goods and services that contribute to their wellbeing.
- Lower income: unemployment benefit is relatively low and wages are pushed down due to a surplus of workers.
- Excluded workers: firms may not want to employ the long-term unemployed, e.g. due to outdated training.
- Lower standard of living: due to less income tax revenue, the government may cut spending on services.
- Tax increases: income tax may increase for those employed if a government needs to raise more money to pay increased benefits.

For government:
- Lower output than potential: one of the factors of production (labour) is not being fully used, so scarce resources are being wasted.

OCR GCSE (9-1) Economics 73

- Budget deficit: the government may spend more than it receives in tax revenue due to increasing costs (such as unemployment benefits) and falling revenue (such as income tax and VAT).
- Costs linked to social problems: these may result from unemployment, e.g. increased health problems due to the unemployed having less money to spend on healthy food.
- Cycle of increasing unemployment: lower incomes lead to lower consumption, leads to less total demand, leads to fewer workers needed to make less output, leads to increased unemployment…

For the regions:
- Differing level of problems: depends on the level of unemployment in an area, e.g. due to the decline of a specific industry a region may have higher costs and need more help from government.
- Regional standard of living: a cycle of increasing negative impacts due to high local unemployment, e.g. shops and services closing.

Exam practice

1 State two types of unemployment. [2]
2 Explain what is meant by unemployment. [2]
3 Explain one method of measuring unemployment. [2]
4 Calculate the unemployment rate if there are 9 million people registered as unemployed and a workforce of 36 million. [2]
5

Table 12.1 UK Unemployment rates, quarterly from January 2008–June 2009

Time period	Unemployment rate (%)
2008 Q1	5.2
2008 Q2	5.4
2008 Q3	5.9
2008 Q4	6.4
2009 Q1	7.1
2009 Q2	7.8

Source: www.ons.gov.uk

Analyse the change in the unemployment rate in Table 12.1. [6]
6 Evaluate whether unemployment is a problem for the government. [6]

Answers and quick quiz 12 online

ONLINE

Summary

You should have an understanding of:
- the meaning of employment and unemployment
- how the Claimant Count can be used to measure unemployment
- how to calculate the unemployment rate
- how to analyse recent and historical unemployment figures
- how to explain the types of unemployment: cyclical, frictional, seasonal and structural
- how to evaluate the causes and consequences of unemployment for individuals, the regions and the government

13 Fair distribution of income

Meaning of distribution of income

- **Distribution of income** is how all the money flowing around an economy is shared between individuals.
- If total **income** is not shared out equally, or is shared unevenly, some people will have high incomes and some will have low incomes.
- The UK has a high level of inequality of income: the top fifth of the population received 40% of total income in 2015.
- Note that total income is measured by GDP in a country.

> **Distribution of income** This describes how income is divided between individuals and households in a country.
>
> **Income** A flow of money over time, often as a reward for use of a factor of production.

Types of income

- Wages: the reward for work. For highly skilled jobs, such as brain surgeons, a limited supply of labour results in a higher wage as hospitals have to compete to attract them.
- Rent: the reward for use of land for a period of time, e.g. renting a house.
- Interest: the reward for saving or lending.
- Profit: the reward for enterprise.
- State benefits: the government transfers income by taxing some people and paying benefits to others, e.g. Jobseeker's Allowance and state pensions. This is not a reward for use of a factor of production.

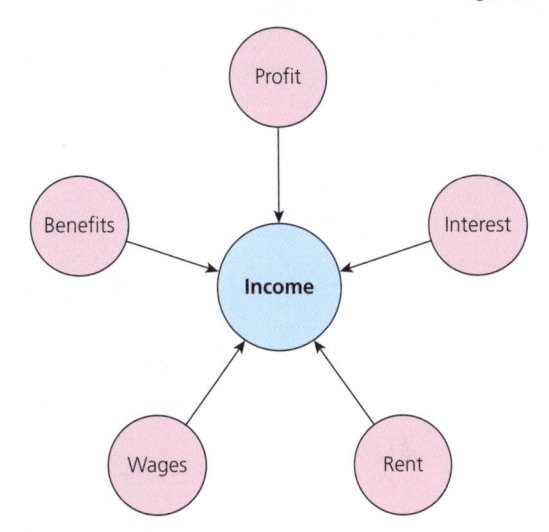

Figure 13.1 Types of income

Difference between income and wealth

- Income is a flow of money over time, e.g. the amount of money an individual earns in a year.
- **Wealth** is the monetary value of assets owned at a specific time, e.g. the total value of all properties owned by a landlord at a point in time.

> **Wealth** The monetary value of all the assets owned by an individual person, firm or country at a specific time.

OCR GCSE (9–1) Economics 75

- Examples of assets that could be valued and contribute to an individual's wealth include houses, cars, antiques, jewellery, savings and shares.
- Income and wealth can be linked, e.g. more income enables individuals to buy more assets, which in turn may lead to greater rewards and income.

Calculation of income and wealth

To calculate income and wealth:
1 Identify whether the items are examples of income or wealth.
2 Split the items into two lists: one for income and one for wealth.
3 Add together all the current monetary values of income – this gives an individual's total income.
4 Add together all the current monetary values of wealth – this gives an individual's total wealth.

Note:
- Gross income or pay is the income before taxes or benefits are taken into account.
- Net income or pay is the income after direct taxes are subtracted and benefits are added.

> **Exam tip**
>
> Remember to use the terms 'wealth' and 'income' correctly in your answers. Wealth is a stock and income is a flow. So an individual may have savings that are a stock and count as wealth, but they generate interest that is income.

Now test yourself

TESTED

1 Calculate total wealth based on the following figures for a household in 2018.

Item	Value
Car	£6,000
Child benefit	£1,600
House	£240,000
Interest from savings account	£132
Wages	£27,000

Answers online

Causes of differences in distribution of income and wealth

Income

REVISED

Some causes of differences in distribution of income include:
- Assets are distributed unevenly: if individuals do not have any land, capital or shares in an enterprise, then they will not receive income in the form of rent, interest or profits.
- Wage differences: wage rates are based on demand and supply for specific jobs, so the equilibrium price varies. Many people may be paid the national minimum wage, whereas for jobs where there is high demand and low supply of labour, the wage rate will be much higher.

- Benefit reliance: state benefits are usually lower than wages and may be the only source of income for a household, e.g. where individuals are pensioners, unemployed or disabled.
- Age: both the young and old are likely to have a lower share of income. People under 25 have a lower level of national minimum wage and younger workers have less experience so are usually paid less. Older people may well be retired and pensions are likely to be less than their previous wage.
- Gender: in the UK, the average income of women is less than that of men. Legally, men and women are supposed to be paid the same for the same work. However, time taken out to look after families or gender bias are cited as reasons for lower pay being given to women.

Wealth

REVISED

Wealth in the UK is distributed more unevenly than income. Causes include:
- Inheritance: some families may own more possessions, e.g. property, which can be passed on to the next generation.
- Savings: some people with enough income may decide to save some of their income rather than spend it all. These savings receive interest and may increase their wealth over time.
- Property: some people with enough income may decide to buy property, e.g. their own homes, property to rent out, or shares in a company. All these types of property can generate income or increase in value.
- Enterprise: entrepreneurs with a business idea may have invested their income or borrowed money to set up a business. A successful business can be worth an increasing amount of money and its increasing value would be a form of wealth.

Consequences of differences in distribution of income and wealth

Costs of inequality

REVISED

- Poverty: in some countries, people without jobs or government benefits may be in absolute poverty so cannot afford to buy the necessities to survive and have less than the minimum standard of living. In other countries, inequality leads to relative poverty where people earn less than 60% of average income, so have a much lower standard of living than other people.
- Housing: people on low incomes may not be able to afford to buy a house or may have to live in poor-quality housing.
- Health: people on low incomes may not be able to afford some healthy food or medicines, so they may be likely to have health problems and a lower life expectancy.
- Education: in countries with no state education, families on low income may not be able to afford education, which can lead to fewer skills, which results in a lower wage and continues the poverty cycle.

- Social problems: the combination of poverty, poor housing, health and education may lead to unhappiness at the unfairness and social unrest within a country.
- Lower economic growth: less-educated, unhealthy and unhappy workers are less productive, so there is less output in an economy.

Benefits of inequality

REVISED

- Incentives: some argue that the possibility of a higher income may motivate people to work harder, which may lead to greater productivity in an economy and its resulting benefits.
- Trickle-down effect: some argue that if some individuals are on higher incomes, they may spend more in an economy or set up businesses, which may lead to more income for other people.

Exam practice

1 The following are all examples of income, except
   A wages
   B interest on savings
   C unemployment benefit
   D property [1]
2 Emma is paid £30,000 for her job in the police. She owns a car worth £10,000 and a flat worth £200,000. She also rents out a room in her flat for £6,000 per year. Her annual income is
   A £36,000
   B £40,000
   C £210,000
   D £246,000 [1]
3 Explain the meaning of distribution of income. [2]
4 Explain one cause of a difference in distribution of wealth. [2]
5 Analyse why households in the UK have different incomes. [6]
6 Evaluate whether the consequences of an uneven distribution of income in an economy are always negative. [6]

Answers and quick quiz 13 online

ONLINE

Summary

You should have an understanding of:
- the meaning of distribution of income, different types of income and the difference between income and wealth
- how to calculate income and wealth
- how to evaluate the causes of differences in the distribution of income and wealth
- how to evaluate the consequences for an economy of differences in the distribution of income and wealth

14 Price stability

Price stability and inflation

- The general price level tracks prices of goods and services in an economy.
- **Price stability** is when the general price level is fairly constant over time.
- **Inflation** is when the general price level increases over time.
- Inflation can lead to a fall in purchasing power, where consumers can buy less with the same amount of money.
- Inflation means the cost of living has increased.
- The rate of inflation is shown as a percentage and is a positive number.
- A negative number would mean that the general price level has fallen over time.

Real and nominal values

- Economists may take inflation into account when comparing information about an economy over time, such as income and the rate of interest.
- A real value takes account of inflation whereas a nominal value does not take this into account.
- For instance, if the rate of interest for a savings account is advertised as 4%, this is the nominal rate of interest. If the rate of inflation is 2.5%, then the real rate of interest is 1.5%.

Measurement of inflation: consumer price index (CPI)

- The **consumer price index (CPI)**:
  - Surveys consumers to create a basket of goods and services that they are buying.
  - Tracks how much they buy of these goods and services so they can give them more importance within the basket – known as weighting.
  - Checks the prices of these goods and services every month.
  - Uses index numbers to show the overall change in this general price level compared to a base year.
- The CPI is set at 100 in the base year.
- Any numbers above 100 show that inflation has risen.

Calculation of the effect of inflation on prices

- If inflation is positive, it means prices are higher (on average) than they were a year ago.

Price stability When the general price level either stays the same or rises at a low rate over time.

Inflation A sustained increase in the general price level.

Exam tip

Inflation means that overall the prices of goods and services have increased. However, it is worth noting that the prices of some goods and services may have fallen.

Real The value of an economic variable that takes account of changes in the general price level over time.

Nominal The value of an economic variable based on current prices.

Consumer price index (CPI) A measure of the general price level used to calculate the inflation rate.

Typical mistake

Take care not to misinterpret a falling inflation rate. As long as the number is positive, the general price level is still rising, albeit at a slower rate.

OCR GCSE (9-1) Economics

- To calculate the change in price due to inflation:

$$\frac{\text{original price}}{100} \times \text{inflation rate}$$

  ○ For example, the effect of a 10% inflation rate on a price of £5.00 would be to increase it by 50p.

$$\frac{500}{100} \times 10 = 50p$$

- To calculate a new price after inflation:

$$\text{original price} \times (1 + \frac{\text{inflation rate}}{100})$$

  ○ For example, if inflation is 10% and the original price is £5.00, this would give a new price of £5.50.

$$£5.00 \times (1 + \frac{10}{100}) = £5.00 \times 1.10 = £5.50$$

> **Exam tip**
>
> Take care to read questions carefully so you answer the exact question set, such as whether the change in price or the final price after inflation is needed.

Now test yourself

1. The price of a pint of milk was 50p in country A in 2018. If the inflation rate is 2.4%, to the nearest whole pence, calculate the change in its price by 2019.
2. The price of a car was £14,000 in country B in 2018. If the inflation rate is 6%, to the nearest whole pence, calculate the new price by 2019.
3. The price of a mobile phone was £300 in 2019. If inflation was 10%, to the nearest whole pence, calculate the price in 2018.

Answers online

Recent and historical data

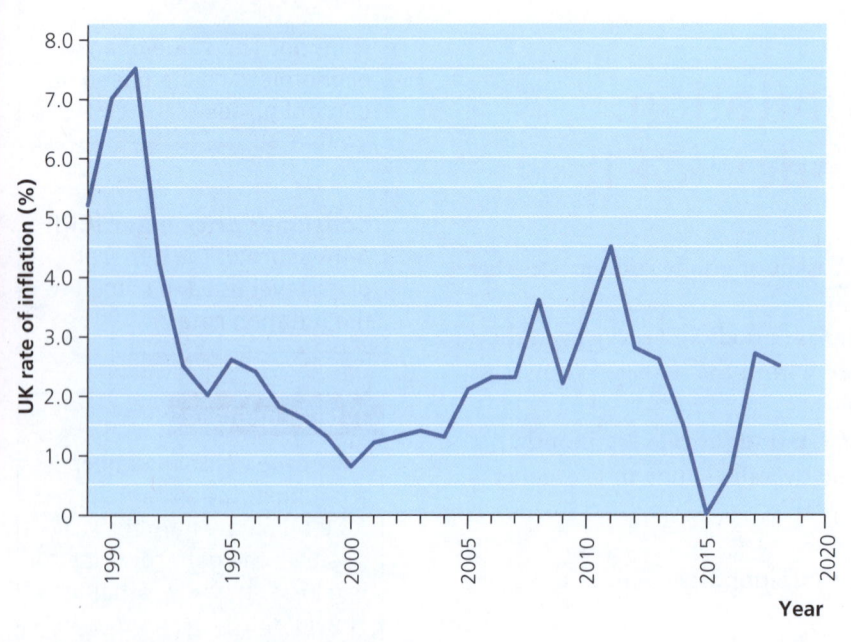

Figure 14.1 UK inflation rates, CPI, 1989–2018

Source: www.ons.gov.uk

- Over the last 30 years in the UK, the inflation rate has risen and fallen with its highest level of 7.5% in 1991.
- The UK had experienced rapid economic growth from the end of the 1980s and this led to demand-pull inflation.

- This was partly caused by an increase in house prices and consumer spending.
- The inflation rate fell after 1991, but has then fluctuated up to 4.5%.
- The inflation rate staged positive, with a lowest rate of 0% in 2015.
- Some of the inflation since 2000 has been caused by cost-push inflation.
- This inflation was partly caused by rising oil prices and higher taxes.

Causes of inflation

Too much demand

- This is also known as demand-pull inflation.
- It happens when total demand rises faster than total supply in a country.
- One cause is increased incomes, because consumers are able to afford more goods and services.
- This means there is increased competition for these goods and services, which leads to higher prices.
- This is more likely where an economy is operating close to its productive capacity because firms are less able to respond easily and quickly to the increase in demand.
- The economy is close to full employment, so it is difficult to find any unemployed workers to produce more output.
- Other causes are rises in investment spending by firms, rises in government spending, increased demand for exports or decreased demand for imports and excess printing of money.

Rise in costs

- This is also known as cost-push inflation.
- This is caused by a rise in costs of production, which firms try to pass onto consumers to maintain profits. This leads to a rise in the general price level.
- Costs of production include: wages and salaries, raw materials, fuel, tax and national insurance contributions, and interest on borrowing.
- A fall in the exchange rate may increase prices of any inputs into production that are imported.
- A fall in productivity leads to a rise in average costs, as a higher proportion of a worker's hourly wage is needed to make a single unit of output, so this increased wage bill increases costs, which leads to higher prices.
- An increase in trade union power may also lead to higher wages being negotiated, which may lead to a rise in inflation.
- A wage-price spiral can worsen inflation as shown in Figure 14.2.

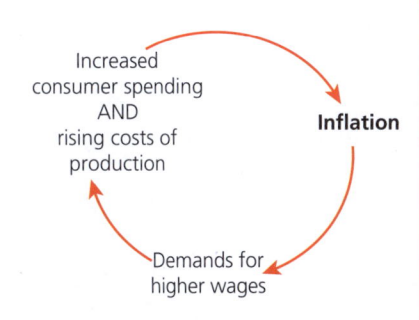

Figure 14.2 The wage-price spiral

Consequences of inflation

Consequences for consumers

- Loss of consumer confidence: inflation makes it more difficult for consumers to value different goods and to decide how to prioritise spending their income, so the uncertainty may stop them buying goods and services.

- Shoe leather costs: as prices change with inflation, consumers and firms have to keep comparing prices of different goods from different suppliers. This costs time and effort to find the best deals, e.g. the highest interest rate on a bank account to balance inflation.
- Fall in real income: if income rises at a slower rate than inflation, consumers will have less purchasing power, i.e. their income will buy fewer goods and services at the higher prices, and their standard of living falls.
- Income redistribution: some workers, e.g. with strong trade unions, may be able to negotiate higher wages during times of inflation so they can maintain or increase their standard of living. However, other workers without this advantage may not get wage increases.
- Consumers as debtors: if consumers have borrowed money, e.g. mortgages, the real value of the debt falls if there is inflation. As the general price level increases, the opportunity cost of paying back the money falls as you can now buy fewer things with the money owed.

Consequences for producers

REVISED

- Increased production costs: inflation may increase the price of inputs, increasing costs and possibly reducing profits.
- Menu costs: firms may have to update pricing information on their goods due to inflation, which can increase their production costs, e.g. printing and distributing new catalogues.
- Labour market disputes: if there is inflation, firms may need to spend more time negotiating wage rises with workers, requiring wages for the negotiators and possibly increased pay for workers.
- Lower exports: if inflation in the UK is higher than in other countries, UK goods may seem relatively more expensive to overseas consumers and they buy less from the UK.
- Producers as creditors: this includes banks who are owed money. If there is inflation, the real value of their loans to borrowers may fall.
- Producers as debtors: firms with debts may gain as the real value of their debt falls.
- Loss of business confidence: if firms are uncertain about the prices of their input costs and the selling price for their goods, this may make them reluctant to invest, which can lead to lower productivity.

> **Typical mistake**
>
> Inflation rate figures can be compared between countries but do not show the actual current general price level. So, although one country may have a higher inflation rate than another, its actual prices may still be lower.

Consequences for savers

REVISED

- If inflation is positive it reduces the purchasing power of money and means that a fixed amount of money can buy fewer goods and services after a period of inflation.
- Inflation reduces the impact of any interest and may reduce the real value of the money saved, for example, if someone is saving for a specific target such as a new car, but the price of the car rises at a faster rate than the person can save.
- The real rate of interest is calculated by:
  nominal rate of interest minus inflation rate

Consequences for government

REVISED

- Government as employer: inflation leads to pressure on the government to increase wages for its employees, such as NHS and state school staff. This can lead to costly industrial disputes and, if wage rises are agreed, increased government spending.

- Government as benefits provider: benefits, such as state pensions and unemployment benefits, may be linked to rise in line with inflation. This means an increase in government transfer payments.
- Tax revenue: if there is inflation, some tax revenue may increase, e.g. VAT and income tax. VAT may increase because it is a percentage of higher prices. Income tax may increase if it is a percentage of higher incomes and people may be dragged into higher tax brackets. However, taxes that are fixed as a specific amount, e.g. tax on alcohol, may fall in real terms.
- Government as debtor: the government borrows money to cover a fiscal deficit. The real value of the national debt can fall if there is inflation, so this may be a benefit for government.

Exam practice

1 Real income could be described as
   A income that does not take into account inflation
   B income that does not take into account benefits received
   C income that takes into account inflation
   D income that takes into account benefits received [1]
2 Explain what is meant by inflation. [2]
3 Explain how inflation is measured. [2]
4 Explain a cause of inflation. [2]
5 Analyse the effects of a high rate of inflation on consumers. [6]
   [Check that you fully understand what is meant by *analyse* before answering this question.]
6 Evaluate the consequences of inflation for a government. [6]

Answers and quick quiz 14 online   ONLINE

Summary

You should have an understanding of:
- the meaning of price stability and inflation
- the meaning of real and nominal values
- how to calculate the effect of inflation on prices
- how to analyse recent and historical inflation figures
- how to evaluate the causes of inflation
- how to evaluate the consequences of inflation for consumers, producers, savers and government

15 Fiscal policy

The purposes of government spending and sources of government revenue

A government needs to raise revenue, largely through taxation, to be able to spend money, mainly on services.

The purposes of government spending

REVISED

A government spends money for many reasons:
- to supply goods and services that the private sector would fail to do, e.g. defence
- to supply goods and services that would be too costly for many people, e.g. healthcare
- to reduce poverty through welfare payments and benefits, e.g. unemployment benefit
- to support the economy when there is insufficient private sector investment/spending.

Type of spending	Purpose of this spending
Social protection	To provide everyone with a basic minimum living standard
	To reduce inequality in income distribution (see Chapter 13)
Education	To provide everyone with education whatever their income
	To ensure that everyone is equipped with basic skills, e.g. reading
Healthcare	To provide everyone with healthcare whatever their income
	To increase the welfare of all, e.g. by preventing diseases
Defence, law and order	To provide essential services the private sector could not do
Debt interest	To repay the money government has borrowed

Government revenue The amount of money the government receives.

Government spending The total amount of money spent by the government in a given time period.

The sources of government revenue

REVISED

Government revenue is the amount of money the government receives from taxes and other sources such as privatisation and is used to finance **government spending**.

Direct taxes

The main **direct taxes** are:

Direct tax	Explanation
Income tax	Paid on all incomes including wages, pensions, dividends etc. Each person gets an income tax allowance before tax is paid
National insurance contributions (NIC)	Paid by both employer and employee
Capital gains tax	Paid on the profit when an asset is sold
Inheritance tax	Paid on the transfer of wealth to relatives when someone dies
Corporation tax	Paid by firms on the profits they have made

> **Direct tax** A tax on income and wealth.
>
> **Indirect tax** A tax on spending which is imposed on the producer but may then be passed on to consumers through an increase in price.

Indirect taxes

The main **indirect taxes** are:

Indirect tax	Explanation
Value-added tax (VAT)	Paid on most goods and services at three different rates: • 20% standard rate applied to the majority of goods and services • 5% reduced rate on, for example, children's car seats and fuel for the home • 0% zero rates on most food and children's clothes
Excise duties	Taxes on specific goods such as alcohol, petrol, tobacco
Customs duties	Taxes on imports of goods into the country

In addition there are other indirect taxes such as:
- insurance premium tax
- landfill tax
- air passenger duties

Now test yourself

TESTED

1 Which of the following taxes are indirect?
   A climate change tax
   B petroleum revenue tax
   C stamp duty
   D student loans

Answers online

Local taxes

In addition to the taxes providing revenue for the UK government, two taxes provide revenue for local authorities:
- council tax, which is a tax on the value of a person's home
- business rates, which are a tax on the value of the property of a business

15 Fiscal policy

OCR GCSE (9–1) Economics   85

Government budgets

The budget shows the revenue and expenditure of the government for the tax year (6 April to 5 April). The budget can be of three different types:
1. **Balanced budget** where the total amount the government is expected to receive in the tax year equals the expected expenditure.
2. **Budget surplus** where the expected revenue is greater than the expected expenditure for the year. The surplus is added to reserves or used to pay off debt.
3. **Budget deficit** where the expected expenditure is likely to be greater than the expected revenue so the government has to use reserves, borrow money (both sensible) or print more money.

> **Balanced budget** Is when revenue is equal to government spending.
>
> **Budget surplus** Is when revenue is greater than government spending.
>
> **Budget deficit** Is when revenue is less than government spending.

Now test yourself

2. Why is printing more money not a sensible option? (See Chapter 14.)

Answers online

Fiscal policy/economic objectives

Remember government objectives consist of:
- economic growth
- low unemployment
- price stability
- improved balance of payments
- fair distribution of income

Fiscal policy

Fiscal policy is the use of taxation and government spending to affect the level of economic activity:
- Budget surplus will reduce economic growth and inflation.
- Budget deficit will increase economic growth and employment.

> **Fiscal policy** A policy that aims to control the economy through the use of government revenue and spending.

How fiscal policy can be used to achieve economic objectives

See the table below for the affects on the five main government objectives.

Objective	Type of budget	Taxation	Spending	Outcome
Rise in economic growth	Deficit	Reduced	Increased	Greater output and employment, perhaps higher inflation and possibly more exports
Lower unemployment	Deficit	Reduced	Increased	More employment and output, perhaps higher inflation/more imports
Price stability, or lower inflation	Surplus	Increased	Reduced	Prices are stable or rise more slowly, balance of payments improves, but growth may fall
Improved balance of payments	Surplus	Increased	Reduced	Imports fall, economic growth may rise as exports exceed imports
Fair distribution of income	Deficit	Increased	Increased	The rich lose income while the poor become better off, both financially and in terms of more services

Remember the opposite will be true if deficit and surplus are swapped around.

How taxes and spending affect markets and the economy

This section will show you how to calculate tax payments and then how to use the information to analyse different situations.

> **Typical mistake**
>
> Candidates often confuse the government's budget and the balance of payments. They are *not* the same.

Taxes

REVISED

Remember these can be either direct (imposed on people) or indirect (imposed on goods and services).

Calculations

Calculations could be for either direct or indirect taxes. Below is an example for each.

Direct: Sian pays tax at the standard rate (20%) on her income of £40,000. If her personal allowance is £12,500, how much tax will she have to pay?

£40,000 − £12,500 = £27,500 which is her taxable pay.

£27,500 × 20% = £5,500. She will have to pay £5,500 in tax.

Indirect: John has been quoted £5,000 excluding VAT for repairs to the drive of his house. If VAT will be charged at the standard rate, how much will the repair cost him?

£5,000 × 20% = £1,000. Total cost is £5,000 + £1,000 = £6,000.

> **Exam tip**
>
> When doing a calculation in Section B of Papers 1 and 2, it is important that you 'show your workings'. There is 1 mark for the working and 1 mark for the correct answer so failing to do this will result in a loss of the mark.

> **Exam tip**
>
> Always make sure you have inserted the unit symbol in the answer, e.g. £.

Analysis

> **Exam tip**
>
> When the exam question asks you to *analyse*, you should demonstrate the ability to present logical chains of reasoning based on knowledge and application. It involves the use of economic terms.

The table shows two examples of how direct taxes could affect both individual markets and the economy.

Tax change	Affect on markets	Affect on the economy
Rise in income tax and NIC	Workers' disposable income falls so they may decide not to work resulting in fall in supply in the labour market Lower income leads to fall in demand especially for non-essential goods and services	Lower demand leads to lower output and economic growth and thus more unemployment. Lower demand leads to lower inflation
Fall in corporation tax	Firms keep more profits so invest more, leading to better quality goods/inventions so demand for those products rise. More people may be needed so the labour market expands	Investment leads to economic growth and more employment. Inventions leads to improved balance of payments

15 Fiscal policy

OCR GCSE (9–1) Economics

The table below shows how indirect taxes could affect both individual markets and the economy.

Type of tax/good	Affect on markets	Affect on the economy
Rise in VAT on TVs	• Fall in demand for TVs • Consumers switch to buying goods with lower VAT	• If produced in UK then employment in the industry will fall. If produced abroad imports may fall • Could be offset by whatever is bought instead of TVs
Rise in excise duty on a good with negative externalities (see Chapter 18)	• Fall in demand for the product, the extent depending on the price elasticity of demand (see Chapter 4) • Could lead to switching, e.g. from petrol cars to electric cars	• Could improve the environment • Could reduce imports, e.g. fall in demand for petrol

Spending

REVISED

As far as the economy is concerned government spending is likely to:
- increase economic growth
- increase employment
- increase inflation
- possibly worsen the balance of payments if there are more imports

The table below shows the effect of government spending on different markets.

Market	Analysis
Labour market	The government is a major employer so any change in spending will have a major effect on: civil servants, teachers, doctors and nurses, etc.
Construction market	Governments are directly responsible for: roads, hospitals and schools. They can also encourage housebuilding by cutting interest rates (see Chapter 16)
Private sector	By building new schools there is more demand for computers, tables etc. so the profits of firms rise. The same will be true if the Royal Navy orders a new ship etc.
Specific markets	Subsidies may be given to specific areas of the economy, e.g.: • renewable energy to replace use of fossil fuels and thus negative externalities (see Chapter 18) • grants for small businesses to encourage new firms in many product markets • grants for firms setting up in areas with high unemployment

The costs and benefits of fiscal policy

- The benefits of fiscal policy means how effective it is in achieving economic objectives.
- The costs of fiscal policy means the what or who the policy has a negative effect on.

The costs of fiscal policy

REVISED

This means not just the actual monetary cost of the policy, but also the unfavourable consequences:
- Consumers may save rather than spend their extra income so the economy does not grow as much as expected.
- Firms and consumers might spend the extra money on imports making the balance of payments worse.
- Inflation may rise if supply cannot keep up with demand in either the factor or product markets (see Chapter 3).

Opportunity cost

REVISED

(If you are not sure about opportunity cost go back to Chapter 2.)
- If the government spends more on one area, e.g. education, then it will spend less on another area, e.g. healthcare.
- If the government spends more it could pay for it by higher taxes. This means consumers have less income so they spend less meaning VAT receipts fall.
- If a government cuts taxes then it must either spend less or accept a higher budget deficit.

The benefits of fiscal policy

REVISED

Benefit	Evaluation
Reduced unemployment	Government can cut taxes/increase spending. There is more demand for labour. Consumers can spend more, so again more labour is demanded
Economic growth increase	Cutting taxes and increasing spending both lead to greater output as consumers purchase more and firms increase investment
Faster acting	Compared with monetary policy (Chapter 16) and supply-side policy (Chapter 17) changes in fiscal policy act more directly and faster on the economy

Economic consequences of measures to redistribute income and wealth

Redistribution involves either direct taxes as these are usually **progressive taxes** (a good example is income tax) or government spending. Governments can also reduce indirect taxes.

The table below shows the income tax rates for 2019-20 for England, Northern Ireland and Wales.

Tax band	Income level (£)
Personal allowance (tax free)	0–12,500
Basic rate (20%)	12,501–37,500
Higher rate (40%)	37,501–150,000
Additional rate (45%)	Over 150,000

Progressive taxes
Taxes that take a greater percentage of tax the higher the income.

OCR GCSE (9-1) Economics

The table below considers some of the consequences of the measures and their outcomes.

Consequence	Evaluation
Reduce inequalities of income	Poorer people are better off and those with higher incomes receive less money
More services available to less well off, e.g. education/health	This increases equality of opportunity so people are in a position to earn more in the future
People may not seek work	If benefits are such that working would not bring in more money, people may opt not to find jobs
Reduces incentives	For those in work getting promoted may mean they have to pay higher taxes so that it is not worth the extra effort
People leave the country	High taxes can lead people to go abroad to where tax rates are lower
Lack of investment	High corporation tax rate can deter firms from investing or they may prefer to invest abroad
Lower savings	If the interest on savings is heavily taxed people may prefer to spend rather than save
Tax avoidance or tax evasion	People may seek ways to avoid paying tax (legal) or try to evade taxes (illegal)

Exam practice

1 To increase economic growth the government would be best advised to:
   A increase government spending and increase indirect taxes
   B increase government spending and decrease income tax
   C reduce government spending and increase corporation tax
   D reduce government expenditure and reduce landfill tax [1]
2 Evaluate the costs and benefits of using fiscal policy to achieve a low level of unemployment. [6]
3 Evaluate the economic consequences of using progressive taxes to redistribute income and wealth. [6]

Answers and quick quiz 15 online

ONLINE

Summary

You should have an understanding of:
- the purposes of government spending
- the sources of government revenue including direct and indirect taxes
- what is meant by a balanced budget, a budget surplus and a budget deficit
- what is meant by fiscal policy
- how fiscal policy can be used to achieve economic objectives
- how to calculate the effect of taxes
- how to analyse the effects of taxation and spending on markets and the overall economy
- how to evaluate the costs, including opportunity cost, of fiscal policy
- how to evaluate the benefits of fiscal policy
- what is meant by progressive taxes
- how to evaluate the economic consequences of measures to redistribute income and wealth

16 Monetary policy

Monetary policy and how it can be used to achieve economic objectives

Monetary policy uses interest rates and other measures, such as quantitative easing, to influence the level of demand in the economy.

Monetary policy

REVISED

Monetary policy is a policy that aims to control the total supply of money in the economy.
- The major objective of monetary policy is a low and stable rate of inflation.
- The Monetary Policy Committee (MPC) of the Bank of England operates monetary policy.
- In the UK, the target is to keep inflation at 2% per annum (+1%/−1%).
- The Bank of England uses its *bank rate* to influence all other interest rates.
- It attempts to limit total demand for goods and services.

> **Monetary policy** A policy that aims to control the total supply of money in the economy to try to achieve the government's economic objectives, in particular price stability.

Monetary policy and economic objectives

REVISED

- The main tool is interest rates.
- In recent years *quantitative easing* has been used to put more money into the economy to encourage consumption and investment.

The way interest rates can work are shown in the table below.

Table 16.1 Summary of how monetary policy changes interest rates to achieve economic objectives

Objective	Interest rates	Effect
Economic growth	Reduced	Increased spending, output and employment
Low unemployment	Reduced	Increased spending, output and employment
Price stability	Increased	Reduced spending, so more price stability
A healthier balance of payments	Increased	Reduced spending including spending on imports

How monetary policy can affect growth, employment and price stability

Monetary policy is used to affect economic growth, employment and price stability. It does not affect the balance of payments directly (see Chapter 20) and is not used to gain a fair income distribution.

> **Exam tip**
> When the exam question asks you to *analyse*, you should demonstrate the ability to present logical chains of reasoning based on knowledge and application. It involves the use of economic terms.

How monetary policy can affect growth

REVISED

Assuming that the rate of interest falls:

Affect	Analysis
Spending and borrowing by consumers increases	Borrowing is cheaper so disposable incomes rise. Spending incurs a lower opportunity cost (less saving). Rising consumption leads to more demand for goods and services and thus increase in total output
Borrowing for investment by firms increases	Again borrowing is cheaper, so firms can increase investment leading to more output
UK exchange rate falls	Lower interest rates lead to an increase in supply/fall in demand for pounds. Exports now cheaper and imports dearer so greater demand for UK goods and services leading to more output

Now test yourself
TESTED

1 Explain one similarity and one difference between fiscal and monetary policies.

Answers online

How monetary policy can affect employment

REVISED

Assuming that the rate of interest falls:

Affect	Analysis
Spending and borrowing by consumers increases	This leads to more demand for UK goods and services so more people are employed to provide these
Borrowing for investment by firms increases	Again this leads to more spending on capital goods so suppliers employ more people. More investment may lead to the growth of firms and thus more employment
UK exchange rate falls	This leads to more demand for UK goods and services and less demand for imports. This means more employment to meet the rising demand

How monetary policy can affect price stability

REVISED

Assuming that the rate of interest rises:

Affect	Analysis
Spending and borrowing by consumers decreases	Borrowing is dearer so those who have a mortgage pay more. Spending incurs a higher opportunity cost (more saving) so consumption falls leading to a fall in demand for goods and services
Borrowing for investment by firms decreases	The cost to firms of borrowing or using their own money for investment rises, so less spending on capital goods. Once again demand falls
UK exchange rate rises	This leads to less demand for UK goods and services and more demand for cheaper imports so overall demand falls

The effects of monetary policy

Although we are treating spending, borrowing, saving and investment separately, there is considerable overlap between them.

The effects of monetary policy on consumer spending

REVISED

- The effect depends on the size of the change.
- The greater the change, the more consumer spending is likely to be affected.
- Large mortgage sector in the UK tends to magnify these effects.

The table below shows the possible effects of a fall in interest rates on consumer spending:

Effect on:	Evaluation
Opportunity cost of spending	This falls so consumers spend more and save less, but see below
Increase in spending	If the fall is large then spending will increase and savings fall, but if small there may be little/no effect
Income	Retired people who rely on income from savings may now spend less as their income falls
Mortgage owners	Those with mortgages now pay less interest so have more disposable income so can spend more

Typical mistake

Although some people lose when interest rates fall (see table), do not apply this to all as most people are better off.

Remember the opposite will be true for a rise in interest rates.

The effects of monetary policy on borrowing

REVISED

- Low interest rates should lead to greater borrowing.
- Banks may be unwilling to lend (as in 2008) so borrowing is more difficult.

The table below shows the possible effects of a fall in interest rates on borrowing:

Effect on	Evaluation
Consumption	Consumers borrow more to buy 'big ticket' items as interest payments are less
Consumer confidence	If consumers lack confidence in the economy a cut in interest rates may not lead to more borrowing
Mortgages	More people can afford to buy houses or to buy larger houses

Remember the opposite will be true for a rise in interest rates.

> **Exam tip**
>
> Make sure you understand the difference between savings and investment. Confusing the two is a common error in exams.

The effects of monetary policy on saving

REVISED

The amount saved should move in the same direction as interest rates. Small changes in the latter, however, may not affect savings.

The table below shows the possible effects of a fall in interest rates on savings:

Effect on	Evaluation
Consumption	This should rise and savings fall as the opportunity cost of consuming is less. Those who depend on income from savings may have to reduce consumption
Fall in price level	If prices are falling then a cut in interest rates may not affect savings as people can consume more due to the price change
Real rate of interest	If the real rate of interest still exceeds the rate of inflation then people may save more as the value of savings is rising

Remember the opposite will be true for a rise in interest rates.

The effects of monetary policy on investment

REVISED

Two sources of money for investment are:
- Loans (see **borrowing** above). Business confidence may counter the change in interest rates.
- Retained profits (see **savings** above).

Other factors affecting investment

- Expected returns from the investment: if these are greater than the rate of interest then firms will invest.
- State of the economy: when an economy is doing poorly this will deter firms from investing whatever the rate of interest.
- Competitors: when competitors are investing it is essential to try to keep up with them by also investing as a firm cannot afford to fall behind despite the change in the interest rate.
- Taxation on profits: high taxes will deter firms from investment.

Exam practice

1. Which of the following shows the best link between monetary policy and economic growth?
   A a reduction in interest rates leading to an increase in output
   B a reduction in interest rates leading to reduced opportunity cost
   C an increase in interest rates leading to greater price stability
   D an increase in interest rates leading to greater government revenue [1]
2. Explain one way in which an increase in interest rates could affect the level of employment in the UK. [2]
3. Evaluate the effects of a rise in interest rates on consumer spending and saving. [6]

Answers and quick quiz 16 online

Summary

You should have an understanding of:
- what is meant by monetary policy
- how monetary policy works
- the effect of monetary policy on economic growth, unemployment, price stability and the balance of payments
- how to analyse the effects of monetary policy on economic growth
- how to analyse the effects of monetary policy on employment
- how to analyse the effects of monetary policy on price stability
- how to evaluate the effects of monetary policy on consumption
- how to evaluate the effects of monetary policy on borrowing
- how to evaluate the effects of monetary policy on saving
- how to evaluate the effects of monetary policy on investment

17 Supply-side policy

Supply-side policy and economic objectives

Whereas fiscal and monetary policies operate on the demand side of the economy, supply-side policies affect the total supply of the economy.

Supply-side policy

REVISED

Supply-side policy is any policy that leads to an increase in the total supply of goods and services in an economy by improving either the quality or quantity of resources. Productive potential is the ability of an economy to supply more goods and services. This often means increasing productivity (see Chapter 8).

The policies and how they can be used are explained below, but there are two important general points:
1 By increasing output they help to reduce inflation without causing unemployment.
2 They only work in the long term so are not a 'quick fix' unlike fiscal and monetary policies.

Supply-side policy Any policy that helps to increase a country's productive potential.

Exam tip

Remember: supply-side policies affect the supply of goods and services *not* the demand. It is fiscal and monetary policies that affect demand.

How can supply-side policies be used to achieve economic objectives?

REVISED

The table below shows some of the main supply-side policies and how they can help achieve economic objectives. The economic objectives are shown in italics.

Supply-side policy	How they help achieve economic objectives
Education and training	Better education and training improves workers' skills and the quality of labour. This increases productivity and *economic growth* (see Chapter 11) and reduces *unemployment* (see Chapter 12)
Competition policy	Control of monopolies increases competition leading to lower prices (*inflation*) (see Chapter 14) and possibly less *unemployment* (see Chapter 12)
Reducing trade union power	This reduces the number of strikes and other industrial disputes leading to higher *economic growth*
Reducing both direct taxes on incomes and benefits	Lower taxes increase the incentive to work as do lower benefits from not working. This reduces *unemployment*
Cutting direct taxes on firms	Cutting corporation tax encourages firms to invest and multinational companies to move to the UK. *Economic growth* and *employment* both rise
Privatisation	Should increase competition leading to greater efficiency and output and lower prices/*inflation*. Exports are more competitive helping to improve the *balance of payments* (see Chapter 20)
Improved transport facilities	Helps to increase the mobility of the factors of production leading to *economic growth* and improved *balance of payments*

> **Now test yourself** TESTED
>
> 1 What are the five economic objectives of governments?
> 2 The table above shows how some of the economic objectives can be affected by supply-side policies. Briefly explain how one or more are affected by each of the policies.
>
> Answers online

The costs and benefits of supply-side policies

- The benefits of supply-side policy means how effective it is in achieving economic objectives.
- The costs of supply-side policy means what or who the policy has a negative effect on.

> **Exam tip**
>
> You may be asked to evaluate either costs or benefits or both. If only costs or benefits you need to decide which ones are more important and which less significant.

The costs of supply-side policies REVISED

Costs	Evaluation
Time lags	Policies take a long time to become effective so the conditions in the economy may have changed
Monetary cost	Because policies take a long time, costs can grow beyond estimates. Policies such as education/training are labour intensive so costly
Opportunity cost	To undertake one policy may involve not doing another, such as spending more on education/training and maybe less on health
Opposition to policies	Policies such as controlling trade unions or monopolies may be unpopular with those affected leading to strikes or less investment respectively
Equity	Cutting benefits may make the poor poorer, at least in the short run
Unintended effects	It is difficult to predict fully the outcome so that a cut in income tax might not lead to people working more as their disposable incomes have risen

The benefits of supply-side policies REVISED

Benefits	Evaluation
Targets specific markets	Policies can be aimed at specific parts of the economy or markets to improve efficiency
Reduced inflation	Product and labour markets become more efficient so output rises to combat increase in demand thus keeping inflation under control
Increased employment	More output requires more workers. Increased productivity can lead to higher wages making working more attractive
Increased economic growth	Policies lead to increased output which leads to economic growth. This in turn is likely to result in higher living standards
Improved balance of payments	Policies leading to increased competitiveness will improve the balance of payments as exports are of better quality and lower priced

> **Typical mistake**
>
> Not evaluating the costs and benefits. It is easy to explain them, but evaluation requires a *supported judgement* which candidates often forget.

Exam practice

1. Which of the following is a supply-side policy?
   A cutting the supply of money
   B increasing government expenditure
   C raising the rate of interest
   D reducing unemployment benefits [1]
2. Evaluate the use of supply-side policies in reducing inflation and increasing employment. [6]

Answers and quick quiz 17 online

ONLINE

Summary

You should have an understanding of:
- what is meant by supply-side policy
- types of supply-side policies
- how supply-side policies can help to achieve economic objectives
- how to evaluate the costs of supply-side policies
- how to evaluate the benefits of supply-side policies

18 Limitations of markets

Externalities

- An **externality** is a cost or benefit from consumption or production for a third party.
- A third party is not involved in either the production or consumption of the good or service.
- The impacts can be positive or negative and can result in external benefits or costs.
- These impacts occur outside of the market transaction.
- Consumers and producers only take into account their own costs and benefits when deciding to trade.
- This means that externalities are not taken into account in market demand and supply.
- The market equilibrium might be wrong resulting in the quantity bought or sold being too high or too low.
- Too many or too few of the country's scarce resources would have been allocated to this good.
- This misallocation is an inefficient use of a country's resources.
- It fails to solve the economic problem, because it is not the best use of limited resources to meet society's unlimited wants.

> **Externality** The impact of an economic transaction on a third party.

Positive externalities

REVISED

- A **positive externality** is a benefit from consumption or production of a good or service on a third party.
- It is also known as an external benefit.
- It has a beneficial effect on someone outside the economic activity.
- For example, a positive externality from production is job creation in other markets, e.g. factory workers may spend their wages in local shops, which creates jobs for third parties outside the factory.
- An example of a positive externality from consumption of education is increased output for third-party firms. People become more skilled, so are more productive.

> **Positive externality** The benefit of an economic transaction for a third party.

Negative externalities

REVISED

- A **negative externality** is a cost from consumption or production of a good or service on a third party.
- It is also known as an external cost.
- It has a harmful effect on someone outside the economic activity.
- For example, a negative externality from production of flights is noise pollution. This has a harmful effect on third-party residents living near airports, who find it difficult to sleep.
- An example of a negative externality from consumption is passive smoking. The decision to smoke creates air pollution that is inhaled by non-smokers nearby, which can harm their health.
- Examples of negative externalities include different types of pollution: land, air, water, visual and noise.

> **Negative externality** The cost of an economic transaction for a third party.

Government policies to correct externalities

- A government may take the view that negative and/or positive externalities have an important impact on society that needs to be taken into account.

Taxation

- **Taxation** tries to work with the market forces of demand and supply.
- A government can correct the existence of negative externalities in a market through taxation.
- **Indirect tax** is a type of taxation that can be added to the price of goods and services.
- One example is 'green taxes', which aim to reduce harm to the environment.
- An indirect tax increases the costs of production for a firm.
- This decreases supply (S to S^1) as producers now have less profit incentive to supply, as shown in figure 18.1.
- This leads to an increase in the equilibrium price (P to P^1) and, in response, quantity demanded falls (Q to Q^1).
- A lower quantity bought and sold should mean there are fewer negative externalities from the economic activity.
- It also mean fewer scource resources are used in production of a good with harmful side effects.
- Taxation on goods with positive externalities can also be set at a lower rate to encourage supply.

> **Taxation** Government collection of money from individuals and firms.
>
> **Indirect tax** A tax raised on spending on goods and services.

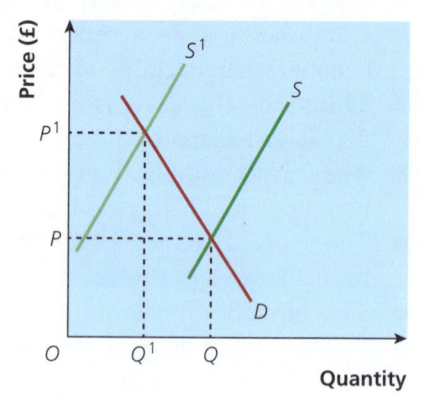

Figure 18.1 The impact of an indirect tax

Taxation to correct externalities

Use and impact

REVISED

- Size of tax: it is difficult to set the correct size of tax to cover the externalities, because they are often difficult to put a price on, e.g. stress resulting from noise pollution. This makes it likely that the tax may not be high enough, so its use has less impact.
- Price elasticity of demand (PED): if PED is inelastic, then consumers are unresponsive to an increase in price, so a tax will create a smaller proportional fall in the quantity demanded than the rise in price, so its use may have minimal impact.
- For example, demand for fast food may be argued to be price inelastic as shown in Figure 18.2 by the steep demand curve.
- The salt and sugar content can make it a habit-forming good.
- There is minimal impact on reducing consumption of fast food from Q to Q^1.
- This suggests the government should consider using other forms of intervention.

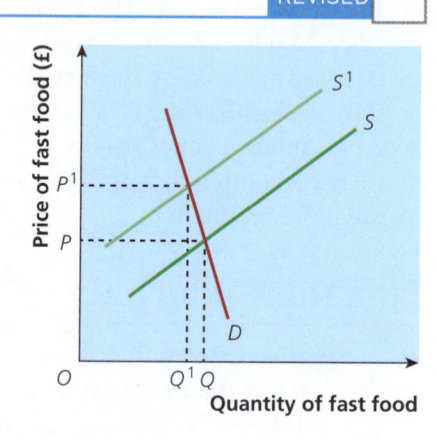

Figure 18.2 The impact of a tax on fast food

Costs and benefits

REVISED

Costs include:
- Tax may be regressive: if the same tax amount is taken, it is a greater proportion of a low income, leaving poor consumers with less income to buy goods and services needed to survive. This may increase inequality.
- Cost to administer and enforce taxation: goods, e.g. cigarettes, may now be sold illegally on the black market, which needs policing. These goods are not regulated, so product safety may be reduced and can have negative effects on health and the NHS. Finally, there is no tax revenue from this unofficial market. This budget impact on government has an opportunity cost for other government services.

Benefits include:
- Reduction in negative externalities as already explained.
- Tax revenue: taxation raises revenue for the government that it can use, e.g. to subsidise goods with positive externalities or to help with problems caused by negative externalities. Tax revenue from goods with inelastic PED can be significant as consumers continue to buy at the higher price.

Subsidies

Subsidies A sum of money given by government to firms to encourage production and consumption.

- **Subsidies** try to work with market forces of demand and supply.
- A government can correct the existence of positive externalities in a market through subsidies.
- The main aim of a subsidy is to encourage production so that more is produced and consumed.
- It may also encourage consumers to switch from goods with negative externalities to those that are subsidised.
- A subsidy decreases the costs of production for a firm.
- This increases supply (S to S¹) as producers now have more profit incentive to supply.
- This leads to a decrease in the equilibrium price (P to P¹).
- In response, quantity demanded rises (Q to Q¹).
- A higher quantity bought and sold should mean the benefits for third parties are now increased.
- It also means a better use of more factors of production for a higher equilibrium quantity.

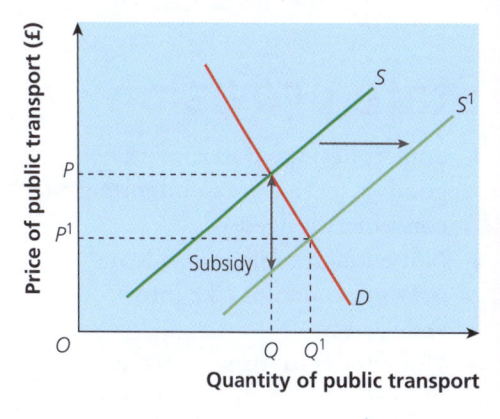

Figure 18.3 The impact of a subsidy

Subsidies to correct externalities

Use and impact

REVISED

- Size of subsidy: it is difficult to set the correct size of subsidy to increase consumption to the level that is best for society. Many of the external benefits are difficult to put a price on, e.g. happiness, so the government may not set the subsidy high enough to have the desired impact.
- Price elasticity of demand (PED): if the aim of a subsidy is to increase production and consumption, then its use on a good with elastic PED will have more impact.
- For example, if demand for broccoli is argued to be price elastic as shown by the flatter demand curve in Figure 18.4.

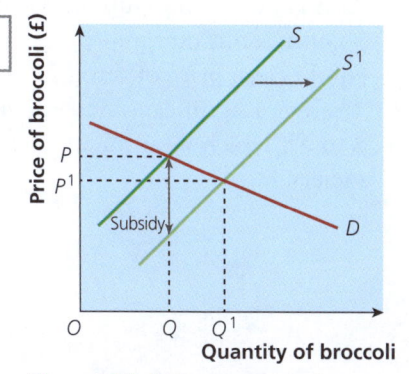

Figure 18.4 The impact of a subsidy on broccoli

OCR GCSE (9–1) Economics   101

- There is a significant impact on increasing consumption of broccoli from Q to Q^1, suggesting the government should use this as a form of intervention.

Costs and benefits

REVISED

- Opportunity cost for government: due to limited resources, if the government pays for subsidies, it may have to give up the benefits of another good or service.
- Opportunity cost for taxpayers: the government may raise taxation to pay the subsidy. Individuals or firms have to sacrifice other uses for the income they lose through tax.
- The main benefit of a subsidy is that it encourages production and consumption of goods with positive externalities.
- It may also lead to more jobs being created in the market subsidised.

> **Now test yourself**   TESTED
>
> Identify the mistakes in the following statements.
> 1 A positive externality is a benefit from consumption or production of a good or service.
> 2 Cigarettes are an example of a negative externality.
> 3 An indirect tax on a good leads to a shift in demand to the left.
> 4 Consumers of petrol are unresponsive when price increases, so petrol is inelastic.
> 5 The main aim of a subsidy is to encourage production and consumption of a good with negative externalities.
>
> **Answers online**

State provision

- Sometimes, the government believes that the benefits for society of a good or service are so important that **state provision** direct to consumers is needed.
- Not enough of these goods and services might be consumed if consumers do not take into account all their benefits for themselves and society.
- Not enough of these goods might be supplied if there is little profit incentive.
- For instance, a government may provide free healthcare so that everyone has access to basic medical help, regardless of whether they can afford it or not. This means there is a healthier workforce who are more productive, which can reduce costs for firms.
- This is shown in Figure 18.5, where the government supplies a fixed quantity of healthcare (S^1) that is free where it meets demand at an equilibrium price of zero.
- There is a significant increase in supply from the free market level of S to S^1, which means many more benefits of healthcare will be seen in society.

State provision Government intervention in a market to supply a good or service direct to consumers.

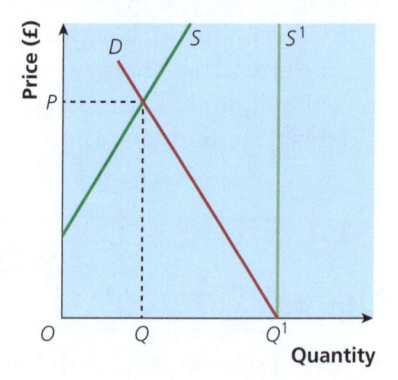

Figure 18.5 The impact of state provision of healthcare

State provision to correct externalities

Use and impact

REVISED

- Difficulty in setting correct level of supply: the impact of state provision depends on whether the government provides enough of the good or service to meet demand.
- If the government supplies too low a quantity of healthcare at S, then when the service is free of charge, Q^1 is demanded but only Q is supplied, as shown in figure 18.6. This means there is excess demand or a shortage, e.g. waiting lists in hospitals.

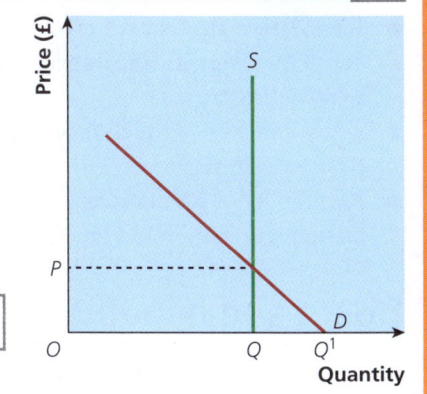

Costs and benefits

REVISED

Costs include:

- Opportunity cost for government: due to limited resources, if the government pays for and provides goods and services for consumers, it may have to give up the benefits of another good or service.
- Opportunity cost for taxpayers: the government uses taxation to raise the funds to pay for state provision. Individuals or firms have to sacrifice other uses for the income they lose through tax. This may be offset by use of free provision of state goods and services.
- Shortages: over time, demand may shift to the right creating or increasing a shortage and making it more difficult for some consumers to access, e.g. due to an increase in population.

Benefits include:

- Improved standard of living: due to the ability for low-income consumers to access essential goods and services.
- Increased benefits for society: there may be many knock-on effects of state provision of certain goods and services, such as education leading to a more skilled workforce, which increases productivity and output.

Figure 18.6 A shortage of free healthcare

Legislation and regulation

- **Legislation** and **regulation** try to change consumer or producer behaviour.
- Some legislation tries to get rid of a market entirely, so there is no demand and supply, e.g. a ban on illegal drugs.
- Regulation targets specific aspects of markets to correct positive or negative externalities.
- There is usually a penalty involved, e.g. a fine, to try to increase the chance of a change in behaviour.
- They can target the externality directly, e.g. stopping the problems associated with chewing gum dropped on the pavement, by fining anyone found dropping it.
- They can try to control the market for a good or service, e.g. age restrictions for drinking alcohol, to try to minimise the negative impacts.
- They can require action, e.g. compulsory attendance at school up to 16 to ensure everyone receives a basic education and can contribute to the workforce.

Legislation A law created by government to control the way individuals or firms behave.

Regulation A rule from the government that firms and/or consumers have to follow.

OCR GCSE (9–1) Economics

Legislation and regulation to correct externalities

Use and impact

REVISED

- Regulation that makes production or consumption of a good illegal can have a significant impact in reducing consumption and negative externalities.
- They can have a much more focused use as they pinpoint specific positives or negatives, rather than just using a price signal.
- Awareness of regulations can increase impact as media coverage may change consumer and producer attitudes.

Costs and benefits

REVISED

- Opportunity cost of policing black markets: there may be significant costs involved in policing unofficial markets for banned goods, but policing is essential to ensure impact. This government money could have been spent elsewhere and any associated benefits are lost.
- Opportunity cost of monitoring regulations: the government may also have to spend money on checking regulations are complied with, such as emissions targets not being exceeded, and penalties are enforced if individuals do not comply.
- The main benefits of regulation are the corrected positive and negative externalities that can benefit society.

> **Information provision**
> Government intervention in a market to give knowledge that might change behaviour.

Information provision

- **Information provision** tries to change the behaviour of economic agents, especially consumers.
- Increased consumption of goods with positive externalities: information may encourage this by giving consumers facts about how the goods benefit themselves and society.
- This may make consumers more willing and able to buy these goods and services, which shifts the demand curve to the right (D to D^1) and increases the quantity consumed (Q to Q^1), as shown in Figure 18.7.
- For example, the '5 A Day' campaign aims to increase consumption of fruits and vegetables, which has health benefits for individual consumers and reduces pressure on the National Health Service.
- Decreased consumption of goods with negative externalities: information provision may discourage consumption by giving consumers facts about how the goods harm themselves and society.
- This may make consumers less willing and able to buy these goods and services, which shifts the demand curve to the left (D to D^1) and decreases the quantity consumed (Q to Q^1), as shown in Figure 18.8.
- For example, the advertising campaigns that the government produces about the harms of smoking should reduce consumption of cigarettes and the health problems for individuals, as well as reducing pressure on the National Health Service.

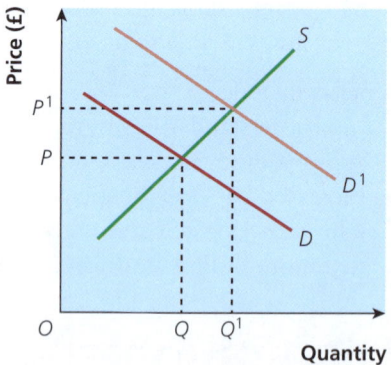

Figure 18.7 Information provision on goods with positive externalities

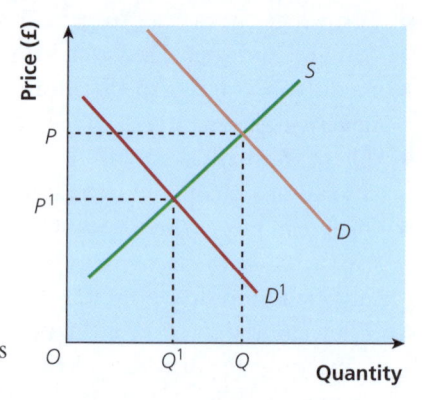

Figure 18.8 Information provision on goods with negative externalities

Information provision to correct externalities

Use and impact

REVISED

- Information provision aims to fill any information gap in the market, which means consumers and producers can make economic decisions when they are fully aware of all the impacts.
- However, consumers may be unresponsive to information, so its provision may be of limited use, e.g. for goods that are addictive.
- There may also be difficulties in delivering the information to consumers, which could limit its impact.

Costs and benefits

REVISED

- Opportunity cost: there are still costs involved with producing and delivering this information, which means the government will not have that money to spend elsewhere.
- However, a benefit of information provision is that it may cost less than other government intervention options, such as subsidies.

Exam practice

1. A positive externality could be described as:
   A a cost from consumption or production of a good or service on a consumer
   B a benefit from consumption or production of a good or service on a third party
   C a cost from consumption or production of a good or service on a third party
   D a benefit from consumption or production of a good or service on a consumer [1]
2. Which of the following is an example of a negative externality of cigarettes?
   A the cost of breathing-related diseases for the consumer
   B the price of the cigarettes
   C the cost of medical treatment for the NHS
   D the cost of production of the cigarettes [1]
3. State two examples of government policies that are used to correct positive or negative externalities. [2]
4. Evaluate the effectiveness of a tax on alcohol to correct negative externalities. [6]
5. Evaluate the impact of information provision about the negative externalities of sugary drinks. [6]
6. Evaluate whether the state should provide free education. [6]

Answers and quick quiz 18 online

ONLINE

Summary

You should have an understanding of:
- the meaning of positive and negative externalities
- how government policies correct positive and negative externalities, including taxation and subsidies, state provision, legislation and regulation, and information provision
- how to evaluate the use and impact of government policies to correct positive and negative externalities
- how to evaluate the costs, including opportunity cost, and the benefits of government policies to correct positive and negative externalities

19 Importance of international trade

- **International trade** is made up of **imports** and **exports**.
- Imports are the goods and services that are purchased from overseas, i.e. producers based in a different country make them. Money flows from the domestic country to the overseas country.
- Exports are the goods and services that a country sells overseas, i.e. domestic producers make and sell them to other countries. Money flows from the overseas country to the domestic country.
- Domestic producers are producers within the home country.

> **International trade** The exchange of goods and services between countries.
>
> **Imports** Goods and services bought from abroad. There is an outflow of money from the domestic country.
>
> **Exports** Goods and services sold abroad. There is an inflow of money into the domestic country.

Reasons for countries to trade

- Different countries have different allocations of resources, i.e. land, labour, capital and enterprise.
- These resources are relatively fixed in quantity over short periods of time, e.g. it takes time to find more oil or to train more workers.
- The different levels of resources can make a country more suited to and relatively more efficient at making particular goods and services.
- This means that countries, and the world, may be better off if each individual country specialises and trades with other countries to get a wider range of goods and services.
- International trade, through specialisation, increases the productive potential of each individual country and encourages economic growth.
- Ongoing trade negotiations resulting from international trade can improve political relationships between countries.
- Specialisation may also mean use of fewer scarce resources globally.
- In other words, international trade may help the economic problem.

Benefits of imports and exports

For consumers:
- Producers need to compete against a wider range of producers internationally, so may reduce price to try to keep or gain market share.
- Producers may respond to increased competition by investing in research and development (R&D) so their goods and services become better quality.
- Consumers now have access to a greater variety of goods, especially goods that countries do not have the resources to be able to produce.

For producers:
- International trade gives access to more potential consumers. With greater output needed to meet this demand, producers may benefit from greater economies of scale. This means they have lower average costs, which may result in greater profits.
- Producers can buy resources for their production worldwide. They can find resources that are not available in their own countries or find resources to buy at lower prices which may lead to lower average costs.

- Increased competition leading to greater efficiency: producers become more focused on how they produce, so they minimise their average costs to compete on price.
- Specialisation and lower average costs: with a greater market, producers can specialise more and grow, leading to more benefits (less wastage of resources during production, increased productivity and output).

Free trade agreements

- The benefits of international trade are only fully received if there is free trade.
- The agreements between member states of the **European Union (EU)** are an example of a **free trade agreement**.
- Protectionism is the opposite of free trade and includes measures governments take to give domestic producers an advantage over imports.
- Free trade agreements mean that the receiving country doesn't impose any restrictions on either imports or exports.
- Examples of restrictions that are lifted are: tax added to imports (tariff) and a maximum quantity of imports allowed (quota).
- So free trade allows specialist producers to sell goods without price or quantity being changed by a country.
- This means consumers may choose to buy lower price (or better quality) goods from these specialists.
- This may benefit consumers as well as reduce use of scare resources globally.
- Countries with a focus on opening up trade and exports, e.g. Hong Kong and South Korea, have experienced greater economic growth than those with more closed economies, e.g. North Korea and Cuba.

> **European Union (EU)**
> An economic and political group of countries in Europe that have free trade with each other.
>
> **Free trade agreement**
> Arrangement to move goods and services between countries without any restrictions.

Now test yourself

TESTED

Identify the terms that fit the following explanations.
1. The exchange of goods and services between countries.
2. Arrangement to move goods and services between countries without any restrictions.
3. Goods and services bought from abroad. There is an outflow of money from the domestic country.
4. An economic and political group of countries in Europe that have free trade with each other.
5. Goods and services sold abroad. There is an inflow of money into the domestic country.

Answers online

The European Union (EU)

- The EU is a group of European countries that have joined together to make a range of agreements that affect their laws and economies.
- This means that there are no import taxes or fixed quantities of imports and exports between EU countries.
- As a result, EU member states, their consumers and producers receive the benefits of free trade within the EU.
- These agreements prevent the occurrence of business practices that reduce competition within the EU, which are considered harmful.
- EU member states agree to a common trading policy with the rest of the world.
- EU member states may also benefit from the EU having more bargaining power with countries in the rest of the world.

OCR GCSE (9-1) Economics

- Any member state leaving the EU will have to renegotiate all trade deals, both with the EU and the rest of the world.
- The outcome of this is uncertain: it will take time to be agreed and take effect.
- Potential departure from the EU immediately creates uncertainty, which can impact an economy negatively, e.g. lower business confidence leading to less investment.

Figure 19.1 EU member states, 2018

Exam practice

1. Which of the following statements is true of free trade?
   A all goods and services are traded free of charge
   B there are no subsidies on goods and services
   C there are no taxes on goods and services
   D there are no limits on quantity of imports [1]
2. Explain what is meant by 'an export'. [2]
3. Explain a benefit of international trade for consumers. [2]
4. Explain a benefit of international trade for producers. [2]
5. Explain an example of restrictions to trade that are lifted by free trade. [2]
6. Explain a benefit from membership of the European Union free trade agreement. [2]

Answers and quick quiz 19 online

Summary

You should have an understanding of:
- why countries import and export goods and services and the benefits of this for consumers and producers
- free trade agreements including the European Union

20 Balance of payments

- The **balance of payments** shows how much a country is spending on imported goods and services, and how successful domestic firms have been in exporting to other countries.
- It is a statement that records all the flows of money coming in and going out of a country.
- Inflows of income from overseas are counted as a positive entry, e.g. exports sold overseas.
- Outflows of income to overseas are counted as a negative entry, e.g. imports bought from overseas.
- The balance of payments is an important measure of the relative performance of the UK in the global economy.

Balance of payments
The record of all financial transactions between one country and the rest of the world.

Balance of payments on current account

- The **current account** is part of the balance of payments and is made up of four main areas: trade in goods, trade in services, income flows and transfers.
- Trade in goods and trade in services are sometimes referred to as 'trade'.
- Trade in goods is the balance of earnings from exports and spending on imports of goods.
  - It used to be known as the visible balance as the goods are tangible, i.e. they can be touched and seen, e.g. agricultural products.
- Trade in services is the balance of earnings from exports and spending on imports of services.
  - It used to be known as the invisible balance, as the services are intangible, i.e. they cannot be touched or seen, e.g. tourism, financial and IT services.
- Income flows are earnings on investments abroad, e.g. interest that foreigners earn in the UK, and that UK nationals earn on investments abroad.
- Transfers are the movement of money or goods and services without any requirement of payment, e.g. foreign aid or money sent 'home' by relatives, so no trade is involved.
- The difference in the monetary value of these four accounts is known as the **balance of payments on current account**.

Typical mistake
Take care not to confuse the balance of payments with the budget balance.

Balance of payments on current account The total of net trade in goods and services, income flows and transfers between one country and the rest of the world.

Current account The record of trade in goods and services, income flows and transfers between one country and the rest of the world.

Balanced current account

REVISED

- A **balanced current account** means that a country's revenue from overseas is the same as its spending overseas.
- The total of negative entries is equal to the total of positive entries.
- The inflow of income matches the outflow of income.
- A balanced current account is unlikely and unnecessary, as other sections of the balance of payments automatically cancel any surplus or deficit.

Balanced current account Where the sum of exports plus the inflow of income and transfers is equal to the sum of imports plus the outflow of income and transfers.

Current account surplus

REVISED

- A **current account surplus** means an economy is consuming less than it is producing in value.
- In other words, a country's revenue from overseas is greater than its spending overseas.
- It is a positive number.

> **Current account surplus**
> Where the sum of exports plus the inflow of income and transfers is greater than the sum of imports plus the outflow of income and transfers.

Current account deficit

REVISED

- A **current account deficit** means that a country is consuming more than it is producing and the income from this extra output is going overseas.
- In other words, a country's revenue from overseas is less than its spending overseas.
- It is a negative number.

> **Current account deficit**
> Where the sum of exports plus the inflow of income and transfers is less than the sum of imports plus the outflow of income and transfers.

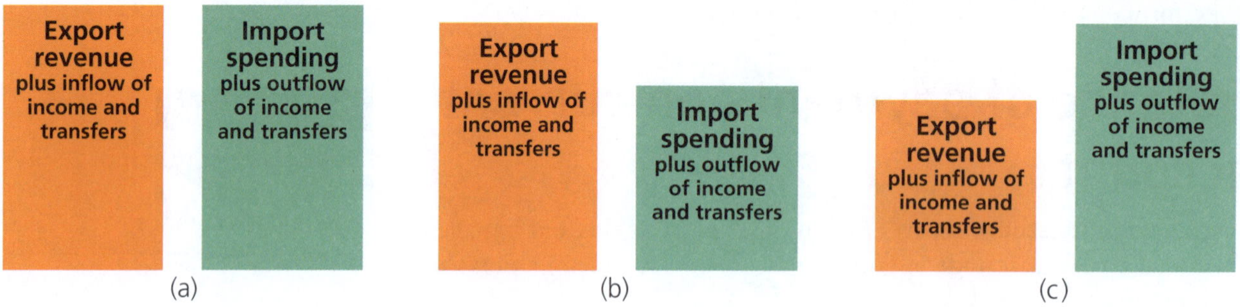

Figure 20.1 (a) Balanced current account, (b) Current account surplus and (c) Current account deficit

Calculation of deficits and surpluses

- The balance of payments on current account is calculated by adding together all the items under trade in goods, trade in services, income flows and transfers.
- If the total is positive there is a surplus.
- If the total is negative there is a deficit.
- Note that the balance of payments on current account is often represented as a percentage of GDP.
- This gives an idea of proportion and how significant a deficit or surplus is.
- It is also a useful measure for comparison between countries.

> **Exam tip**
> Take care in all calculations questions to check that you have used the correct currency (e.g. $ or £) and the correct multiples (e.g. billions or millions).

Now test yourself

TESTED

1 Calculate the balance of payments on the current account and identify whether there is a surplus or deficit for each country.

	Country A	Country B	Country C
Trade in goods (£bn)	−20.3	+34.1	−6.9
Trade in services (£bn)	+14.5	+12.8	−12.1
Income flows (£bn)	+6.1	−8.1	+13.6
Transfers (£bn)	−8.3	−12.6	−6.7

Answers online

Recent and historical data

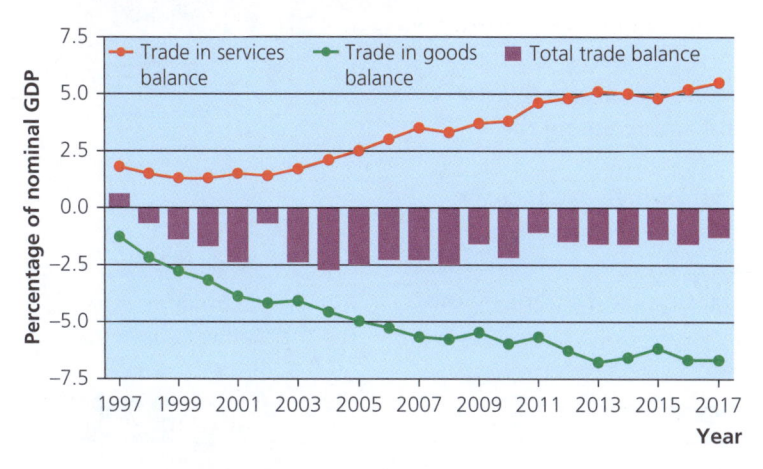

Figure 20.2 The balance of trade in goods and services in the UK, 1997–2017 (% of GDP)

- Figure 20.2 shows that between 1997 and 2017 the deficit of the UK trade in goods increased by 5.4% of GDP.
- This means that imports of goods have increased more than exports of goods.
- The surplus of the UK trade in services mostly increased.
- The overall trade balance deteriorated, from a small positive balance in 1997 of 0.5% of GDP to a negative balance of about 1.3% of GDP in 2017.
- The trade deficit slightly reduced in 2016 to 2017, from -1.6% to -1.3% of GDP.
- Since 1998, the trade in services surplus has been less than the trade in goods deficit, so overall there has been a deficit in trade.
- Exports to the EU have fallen, partly due to lower demand for UK goods in the EU, possibly as a result of weakening economies in some parts of the EU.
- Imports to the UK have increased, partly due to an increase in UK demand for imports of oil, gas and consumer goods.

The importance of the current account to the UK economy

The importance of a current account deficit

REVISED

A deficit is of particular importance and concern:
- If it is caused by problems in the economy, such as falling total demand for domestic goods, which can be caused by low international competitiveness and poor product quality.
- If it is due to a factor that will take a long time to change, such as low productivity, as the deficit will last longer which is harder for the country to be able to finance.
- If it is large in size as again this is harder for a country to be able to finance and increases national debt more significantly. It also has bigger consequences such as higher unemployment.
- The country may then need to take action that is harmful such as cutting other government spending, which could have an opportunity cost.

20 Balance of payments

OCR GCSE (9-1) Economics 111

Alternatively, the deficit may not be so important or a concern if:
- It is only temporary, e.g. due to importing more raw materials or capital goods to put into the production of goods that will eventually be exported and increase economic growth.
- It reduces inflation within the domestic economy: imports are greater than exports, thereby decreasing total demand and reducing the upwards pressure on prices.
- Over time, it leads to a fall in the exchange rate, which can increase the international competitiveness of UK goods and eventually increase exports.
- It is only a small percentage of GDP so the debt can be paid for by the country with less difficulty.

The importance of a current account surplus

REVISED

A surplus is of importance and benefit if:
- It reflects rising total demand for domestic goods, which can be linked to decreased unemployment, more income tax revenue and lower benefit payments.
- It decreases the debt of a country because more money is flowing into the country from greater spending on exports than money is flowing out to pay for imports.

Alternatively, the surplus may not be important or a benefit if:
- It causes rising inflation within the domestic economy: as exports are greater than imports, thereby increasing total demand for domestic products and putting upwards pressure on prices.
- It hides the causes that have a negative impact on global economic growth such as protectionist policies that give domestic goods an artificial advantage.
- It leads to a rise in the exchange rate, which can decrease the international competitiveness of UK goods and eventually decrease exports.

Causes of surplus and deficit of the current account

Causes of a surplus

REVISED

- The strength of the economy, e.g. products are of a high quality, sold at a low price, or reflect what households and firms at home and overseas want to buy.
- A lack of growth in the domestic economy: consumers within the economy may buy fewer imports, while domestic firms, finding it difficult to sell at home, compete more to sell exports abroad.
- A fall in the exchange rate, which may increase the quantity of exports if overseas consumers are responsive to the now lower export prices. It may similarly reduce imports.
- A net inflow of investment income: investments that foreign residents have made in the country earn less than the investments the country's inhabitants have made in other countries.

Causes of a deficit

REVISED

- Structural problems in the economy, e.g. firms overpricing goods, producing poor-quality goods or goods no longer in demand.
- Falling incomes overseas, which may lead to falling exports.
- Rising incomes in the domestic economy may lead to rising imports.
- A rise in the exchange rate, which may decrease the quantity of exports if overseas consumers are responsive to the higher export prices. It may similarly increase imports.
- A net outflow of investment income: the investments that foreign residents have made in the country earn more than the investments the country's inhabitants have made in other countries

Exam practice

1. Which one of the following is a component of the current account of the balance of payments?
   A government tax revenue
   B trade in services
   C government spending
   D the capital account [1]
2. Explain what is meant by a deficit on the current account on the balance of payments. [2]
3. Explain one cause of a deficit on the current account of the balance of payments. [2]
4. Explain one cause of a surplus on the current account on the balance of payments. [2]
5. Evaluate whether a fall in the value in the pound to the euro exchange rate might affect the UK's current account on the balance of payments. [6]
6. Evaluate the importance of a deficit on the current account on the balance of payments. [6]

Answers and quick quiz 20 online

ONLINE

Summary

You should have an understanding of:
- the balance of payments on current account
- the meaning of a balanced current account, a current account surplus and a current account deficit
- how to calculate deficits and surpluses
- how to analyse recent and historical data on exports and imports
- how to evaluate the importance of the balance of payments on current account to the UK economy
- how to evaluate the causes of surpluses and deficits on the balance of payments on current account

21 Exchange rates

- Most countries have their own currency, so to allow trade between countries it has to be possible to buy one **currency** using another.
- This allows economic groups in one country to buy goods in another country with that country's currency, using an **exchange rate**.

> **Currency** The system of money used in a country or group of countries.
>
> **Exchange rate** The price of one currency in terms of another currency.

Drawing and analysing exchange rate diagrams

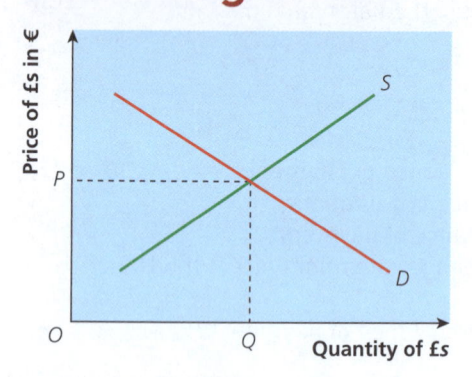

Figure 21.1 The exchange rate for pounds in terms of euros

- The exchange rate for a currency is set at the equilibrium of demand and supply, where $D = S$ at a price of P in Figure 21.1.
- This equilibrium price shows the external value of a currency.
- It shows how much of another currency it can buy.
- The demand curve (D) is the demand for pounds: mostly from overseas economic groups who want pounds to buy British goods, services and financial assets from the UK.
- The supply curve (S) is the supply of the pound: mostly from UK economic groups who supply their pounds in exchange for another currency to buy goods, services and financial assets from other countries.

> **Exam tip**
>
> Note: the y-axis of an exchange rate diagram is the price of the currency that is demanded and supplied in terms of the other country's currency, e.g. 'price of £s in €'.

A rise in the exchange rate

REVISED

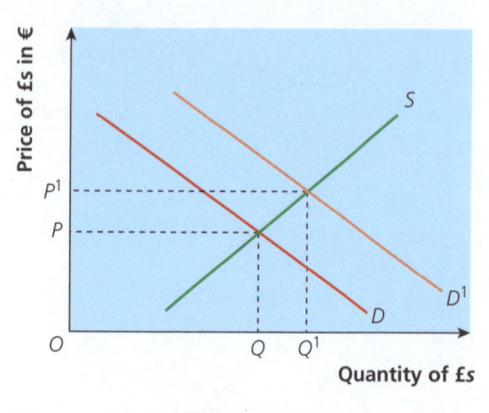

Figure 21.2 A rise in the exchange rate due to an increase in demand for £s

- A rise in the exchange rate means the price of a currency increases in terms of another currency.
- This is also referred to as the currency becoming stronger or as an appreciation of the currency.
- There are two possible changes that lead to a rise in the exchange rate: an increase in demand for a currency or a decrease in supply of the currency.
- Figure 21.2 shows the effect of an increase in demand for pounds: the demand curve shifts right (D to D^1), the price of the pound increases (P to P^1) and quantity traded rises (Q to Q^1).
- The exchange rate rises, e.g. the price of the pound at P may have been £1 = €1, whereas after the increase in demand, it might increase to £1 = €2.
- Each pound now buys more euros and more euros have to be sold to buy a pound.

> **Exam tip**
>
> Note: demand and supply in an exchange rate diagram work the same as in other market diagrams. An increase in either demand or supply results in a shift to the right ('right is a rise'). A decrease in either demand or supply results in a shift to the left ('left is lower').

A fall in the exchange rate

REVISED

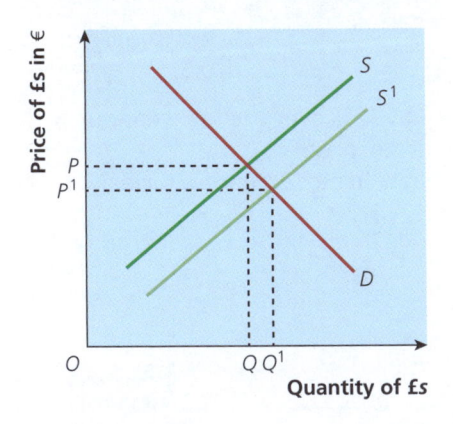

Figure 21.3 A fall in the exchange rate due to an increase in supply of £s

- A fall in the exchange rate means the price of a currency decreases in terms of another currency.
- This is also referred to as the currency becoming weaker or as a depreciation of the currency.
- There are two possible changes that lead to a fall in the exchange rate: a decrease in demand for a currency or an increase in supply of the currency.
- Figure 21.3 shows the effect of an increase in the supply of pounds: the supply curve shifts right (S to S^1), the price of the pound decreases (P to P^1), and quantity traded rises (Q to Q^1).
- The exchange rate falls, e.g. the price of the pound at P may have been £1 = €2, whereas after the shift of the supply curve, it decreases to £1 = €1.
- In effect, each pound now buys fewer euros, and fewer euros have to be sold to buy a pound.

> **Exam tip**
>
> To analyse how the exchange rate is determined, you need to be able to explain the factors affecting demand and supply and the effect on the exchange rate diagram using logical chains of reasoning.

> **Typical mistake**
>
> In exams, you will need to read the question carefully so that you use the correct currencies on your diagram.

Factors affecting demand for pounds

REVISED

Economic groups in other countries, e.g. in the eurozone, need pounds for four key reasons:
1 to buy UK exports of goods and services
2 to save in UK bank accounts
3 to speculate on the pound (known as flows of 'hot money')
4 to invest in the UK

OCR GCSE (9–1) Economics 115

For instance, demand for the pound may increase because:
- UK goods become more desirable: e.g. due to a fall in price if the inflation rate in the UK falls relative to that in other countries.
- Incomes rise in the eurozone, so eurozone consumers can now afford to buy more goods, and this is likely to include UK exports.
- Interest rates in the UK rise relative to other countries' interest rates, so eurozone savers would want to save more in the UK to take advantage of the increased reward.
- Corporation tax falls in the UK, so overseas producers want to set up businesses and trade from the UK as a base.
- Some eurozone speculators think the value of the pound will rise in the future so it is worthwhile buying the pound now to exchange for more euros in the future.

These scenarios would all result in the effect seen in Figure 21.2.

> **Typical mistake**
>
> Note: take care when using the word 'change' in exams. This can be too vague to gain marks, so consider whether increase/decrease or rise/fall might be better.

Now test yourself

TESTED

Identify the impact on the demand curve for pounds in the following scenarios:
1 The interest rate in the UK increases by 3%.
2 There is a news story suggesting that British meat is not safe to eat.
3 An independent report says that productivity in Britain has increased by 12% over the last year.
4 The government announces an increase in corporation tax (a tax on firms' profits).
5 It is reported that most of the overseas car producers in the uk are likely to close their factories by 2024.

Answers online

Factors affecting supply of pounds

REVISED

British economic groups need other currencies, e.g. euros, so will trade pounds for four key reasons:
1 to buy imports of EU goods and services
2 to save in eurozone bank accounts
3 to speculate on the euro (known as flows of 'hot money')
4 to invest in the eurozone

Therefore, supply of the pound may increase because:
- Eurozone goods become more desirable, e.g. due to a fall in price.
- Incomes rise in the UK, so British consumers can now afford to buy more goods, and this is likely to include imports.
- Interest rates in the eurozone rise, relative to other countries' interest rates, so British savers would want to save more there to gain the increased reward.
- British speculators think the value of the euro will rise in the future so it is worthwhile buying the euro now to exchange for more pounds in the future.
- Productivity rises in the eurozone, so UK producers want to set up businesses and trade from the eurozone as a base.
- The eurozone becomes more attractive for foreign investment, e.g. due to a reduction in regulations.

These scenarios would all result in the effect seen in Figure 21.3.

Table 21.1 Summary of exchange rate changes: diagrams and causes

Change in the exchange rate	Change in demand or supply of £s	Change on diagram	Example of cause
Rise	Decreased supply of £s	Supply curve shifts left	Fewer imports bought from eurozone
Rise	Increased demand for £s	Demand curve shifts right	More exports sold to eurozone
Fall	Increased supply of £s	Supply curve shifts right	More imports bought from the eurozone
Fall	Decreased demand for £s	Demand curve shifts left	Fewer exports sold to eurozone

Calculation of currency conversion

- These are methods for calculating a currency conversion, using British pounds (£) and euros (€) and an exchange rate of £1 = €1.20.
- To convert pounds into euros: multiply the amount in pounds by the exchange rate.
  - For example, to convert £5.70 to €:

  £5.70 × €1.20 = €6.84

- To convert euros into pounds: divide the amount in euros by the exchange rate.
  - For example, to convert €3.45 to pounds:

  €3.45 ÷ €1.20 = £2.88

> **Now test yourself**   TESTED
>
> 6 A student going on an exchange to Germany wants to exchange £80. The current exchange rate is £1 = €1.20. How many euros will she take to Germany?
> 7 A sports car is for sale in America for $24,000. If the exchange rate is £1 = $1.30, what is the price of the car to the nearest whole pound?
> 8 Grandparents want to buy a gift voucher for a French sports shop for €50 for their grandchild who lives in France. The current exchange rate is £1 = €1.20. How much will this cost them to the nearest whole penny?
>
> Answers online

Recent and historical data

- The UK's exchange rate can be analysed in terms of any other currency.
- Figure 21.4 plots how many US dollars are converted to make a British pound.

Figure 21.4 The number of US dollars per British pound, 2008–18
Source: www.bankofengland.co.uk

- The highest point of needing US$1.85 to buy a single pound was recorded in 2008. This reflected concerns about the US economy and big problems in their banking industry.
- The exchange rate then fell until March 2009. This reflected greater uncertainty and growing problems in banking in the UK.
- The exchange rate then rose a little and stayed at a similar level with smaller fluctuations through to 2015.
- The stability of the exchange rate at this lower level reflected the relatively slow growth in the UK economy over this period.
- The exchange rate fell overall during 2016 following uncertainty about the impacts of Brexit and leaving the European Union.
- Albeit with some fluctuations, the exchange rate then stayed around this lower level of between US$1.29 and US$1.34 to 2018.

The effect of changes in the exchange rate

Effect on consumers

After a rise in the exchange rate:
- Import prices fall: domestic consumers may be more willing and able to buy imported goods.
- An improved standard of living: domestic consumers may enjoy a better standard of living as their income can buy more imported goods. This depends on the type of good imported.
- Increased tourism overseas: more domestic consumers may go overseas for holidays as their British pound will buy more foreign currency.
- A fall in the inflation rate: due to total demand falling, if imports grow and exports fall, there is likely to be a downward pressure on the price level. This may benefit consumers, as their income will now, in effect, buy more goods.

Exam tip

Take care to refer to specific countries and their currencies if this is relevant to the question set.

Effect on producers

REVISED

After a rise in the exchange rate:
- A fall in import prices: this is a benefit for producers who import raw materials, components or capital goods, as now their average costs will be lower and there is a chance of increased profits.
- Increased tourism overseas: producers involved in the provision of holidays overseas, e.g. travel agents and airlines, should benefit from the increased demand from British consumers. However, producers involved in providing holiday and leisure services within the UK may suffer.
- A rise in export prices: usually this would be expected to result in a fall in demand for goods from British producers, which may mean lower profits or losses leading to firms shutting down. However, if overseas consumers have inelastic PED for these British goods, they will not be responsive to the rise in price and may still continue to demand a similar quantity.
- A fall in the inflation rate: due to total demand falling, if imports grow and exports fall, there is likely to be a downward pressure on the price level. This may benefit producers, as there is less need for wage rises, it should lower menu costs and British products become more internationally competitive.

Exam practice

1 If the exchange rate is £1 = €1.20, which of the following is a correct conversion of £360?
   A £432   B £300   C €300   D €432   [1]
2 Explain what is meant by the term 'exchange rate'. [2]
3 On the diagram below:
   - Draw and label a new demand curve to show the effect of a fall in the quality of the UK's goods.
   - Label the changes in the exchange rate of the pound sterling and in the quantity of pounds. [2]

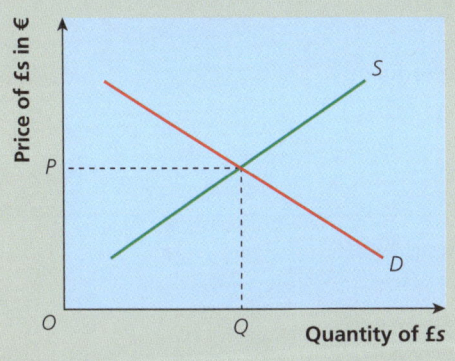

4 Explain an impact of a rise in the exchange rate on UK consumers. [2]
5 Explain one way a decrease in a country's interest rate is likely to affect its exchange rate. [2]
6 Evaluate whether a fall in the exchange rate for UK producers is beneficial. [6]

Answers and quick quiz 21 online

ONLINE

Summary

You should have an understanding of:
- how to draw exchange rate diagrams
- how to analyse how exchange rates are determined through the interaction of supply and demand
- how to calculate currency conversion
- recent and historical exchange rate data
- how to evaluate the effect of changes in the exchange rate on consumers and producers

22 Globalisation

The meaning of globalisation

- **Globalisation** is the interdependence of countries due to international trade.
- There is now more freedom of movement of goods, services, people and money through different countries.
- There is increasing global sourcing: almost any good can be made anywhere in the world using resources from anywhere else.
- These goods can then be sold anywhere and the resulting profits equally could go anywhere in the world.
- Globalisation can be seen in the existence of global brands such as McDonald's and Coca-Cola.

> **Globalisation** Integration of countries through trade.

Driving factors of globalisation

Reduction of barriers to international trade

- At various points in time, such as after the Second World War, countries had to work together and trade with each other in order to grow their economies.
- This resulted in the removal of barriers to trade such as taxation and regulations that restricted movement of resources.
- This led to easier movement of people, raw materials, money and goods between different countries.
- The costs associated with barriers to international trade were reduced and it became more profitable to trade around the world.

Improvements in transport

- Improvements in transport have enabled producers to trade worldwide: to source and buy inputs for production and also to distribute goods around the world.
- This has enabled firms to trade worldwide by employing overseas producers to take on parts of the production process.
- Improvements have cut the average costs of transport, e.g. development of huge container ships has resulted in economies of scale for transport, making it more profitable to trade worldwide.
- They have cut transport time, making it possible to trade goods worldwide that might otherwise have perished on longer journeys.
- Investment into transport infrastructure worldwide has made it possible for goods and people to travel between countries, so greater integration and trade worldwide is more likely to happen.

Worldwide foreign investment

REVISED

- Foreign investment is now a significant contributor to the flow of money into and out of different countries and has increased the interdependence of countries around the world.
- The promotion of free trade and the removal of restrictions on foreign investment have ensured significant growth.
- For example, China has had a balance of payments surplus and has used this to invest overseas.
- China is now the second-largest overseas investor in the UK, after the USA.
- The growth of multinational corporations (MNCs) has also resulted in an increase in worldwide foreign investment.
- These businesses, such as Shell and Nestlé, have a base in one country but will then conduct business (via production or retail outlets) in other countries.
- In order to produce or sell in another country, these businesses have to invest in all sorts of ways, from buying factories to building roads.
- This network of MNCs can significantly increase world trade and the integration of countries worldwide.

Advances in technology and communications

REVISED

- Advances in technology and communications have made it both easier and less costly to trade around the world.
- It is easier for producers to have parts of their business in other countries, e.g. accounts and IT departments.
- The internet has allowed producers to find suppliers of the resources they need for production in different parts of the world, thereby increasing trade.
- It has enabled consumers to find a wider range of suppliers and products from countries around the world that can now be traded.
- Online banking and e-commerce have made buying and selling worldwide faster, more secure and easier, which has encouraged the expansion of trade globally.

Measurement of development

Development is measured by key indicators of standard of living and wellbeing:

- GDP per capita: an increase in GDP represents economic growth, where more workers are paid to make increased output. This means they can afford to buy more and improve their standard of living.
- Life expectancy: this is the average age to which a person lives and is a useful gauge of development – it is likely to tally with the overall health of a population and reflects the standard of living.
- Access to healthcare: the availability of hospitals, medical facilities and medical professionals has a significant effect on wellbeing.
- Technology: statistics on access to technology, e.g. mobile phones and internet, link to education, enabling communication and trade, and personal banking services that help individuals prosper.

Development The process of increasing people's standard of living and wellbeing over time.

- Education: numbers accessing education and the literacy rate, i.e. percentage of adults who can read and write. Education increases future productivity and economic growth. It can reduce inequality in a country as an increase in skills enables people to access higher wages and standard of living.

> **Now test yourself** TESTED
>
> Identify whether development might increase or decrease based on the following scenarios.
> 1 Ownership of mobile phones has increased by 20%.
> 2 The number of doctors in a country falls as some migrate to jobs in other countries.
> 3 The number of personal bank accounts increases by 30%.
> 4 The average age for men to live to in a country falls from 78 to 72.
> 5 GDP increases by 10% as population increases in 4%.
>
> **Answers online**

Costs and benefits of globalisation

Impact in developed countries REVISED

- Developed countries are countries that have reached an advanced stage of development.
- Economic indicators include: high GDP per capita and developed industrial and service sectors.
- Human indicators include: high levels of education and healthcare.

Developed country
A country with high GDP per capita and established industry and service sectors.

Producers

Costs include:
- Possible decline of industry: less developed countries may have a cost advantage, such as low wages, which means producers in developed countries are unable to compete and have to close.
- Vulnerability to problems in the worldwide economy: e.g. if incomes fall in another country, producers in developed countries are not able to export as much, which may harm businesses.
- Some increased production costs: e.g. increased administration costs to enable trading across the world, e.g. paying lawyers in different countries and set-up costs for facilities overseas.

Benefits include:
- Wider markets to sell into: the potential for vastly increased sales as producers can now sell virtually anywhere in the world, which could lead to greater economies of scale or specialisation.
- Cheaper and wider range of resources: the ability to buy resources worldwide increases competition meaning lower prices, as well as access to resources that were not available in their own country.
- Cheaper and more skilled labour force: increases in overseas workers can benefit producers who have access to a wider range of workers, sometimes with different skills or willing to work at lower prices.

Workers

Costs include:

- Decline of industry and structural unemployment: industries may go into decline due to global competition and it may be difficult to get new jobs requiring new skills.
- An increase in the use of machinery and unemployment: there may be fewer jobs if, in a bid to be more internationally competitive, producers replace workers with machinery to increase productivity.
- An increase in dependence on world markets and unemployment: e.g. if incomes fall in other parts of the world, the demand for UK goods may fall, so fewer workers are needed to make less output.
- An increase in immigration and unemployment: more immigration may have a negative effect for workers in the domestic country if they are not competitive in terms of either skills or price.

Benefits include:

- Increased employment due to increased output: over time, there may be more jobs available as the economy produces more to meet the demands of international trade.
- Increased employment due to increased foreign investment: this can lead to more jobs being created in new businesses that are formed.
- Increased geographical mobility: the opening up of markets means that workers from developed countries have the opportunity to live and work anywhere in the world.

Consumers

Costs include:

- Rising prices: as there are more consumers competing to buy some goods, this can actually lead to an increase in worldwide prices.
- Less choice due to global brands: e.g. the rise of global companies like Starbucks may have led to smaller, local coffee shops closing.
- Volatile prices: if prices fluctuate greatly on goods traded globally, such as oil, it can lead to worldwide uncertainty and difficulty planning personal finances.

Benefits include:

- A wider range of goods: in general consumers are able to research and buy a wider range of goods from around the world.
- Lower prices for goods: increased worldwide competition between firms should result in lower prices, increasing affordability and standard of living
- Better-quality and more innovative goods: due to increased competition, producers have to be much more focused on the quality of their goods and innovate to stay ahead of rivals worldwide.
- Greater opportunity to travel: opening up borders allows greater tourism and travel for consumers in developed countries.
- Improved services due to more skilled professionals: due to freer movement of people, there may be more skilled professionals moving from less developed countries to developed countries.

> **Exam tip**
>
> When answering a question on costs and benefits of globalisation, take care to answer the exact wording of the question, e.g. if you are asked to focus on a specific aspect.

Economic, social and environmental sustainability

Economic sustainability:
- Initially, globalisation can have a negative economic impact. If an industry is less efficient than in other countries, it cannot compete on price, which can lead to the decline of the whole industry in the developed country, which results in unemployment and knock-on effects for the economy.
- Over time developed economies should adjust production to more profitable activities where they have greater efficiency than less developed countries, e.g. services and high-tech industry. They can also benefit from lower costs by international trading of resources needed. This should result in positive impacts, such as increased GDP, less unemployment and greater tax revenue.

Social sustainability:
- The benefits of more and lower-priced goods for consumers contribute significantly to an increased standard of living within developed countries.
- However, if there is increased unemployment, leading to lower income, less ability to afford goods and services leading to a lower standard of living, this can create much hardship in society.

Environmental sustainability:
- Globalisation may have a positive impact through increased international trade, because countries should specialise in the goods they can produce most efficiently and use the fewest resources.
- However, if there are environmental problems due to globalisation and industrial practices in less developed countries, such as pollution and resource usage, if allowed to continue, these may impact on the rest of the world, including developed countries.

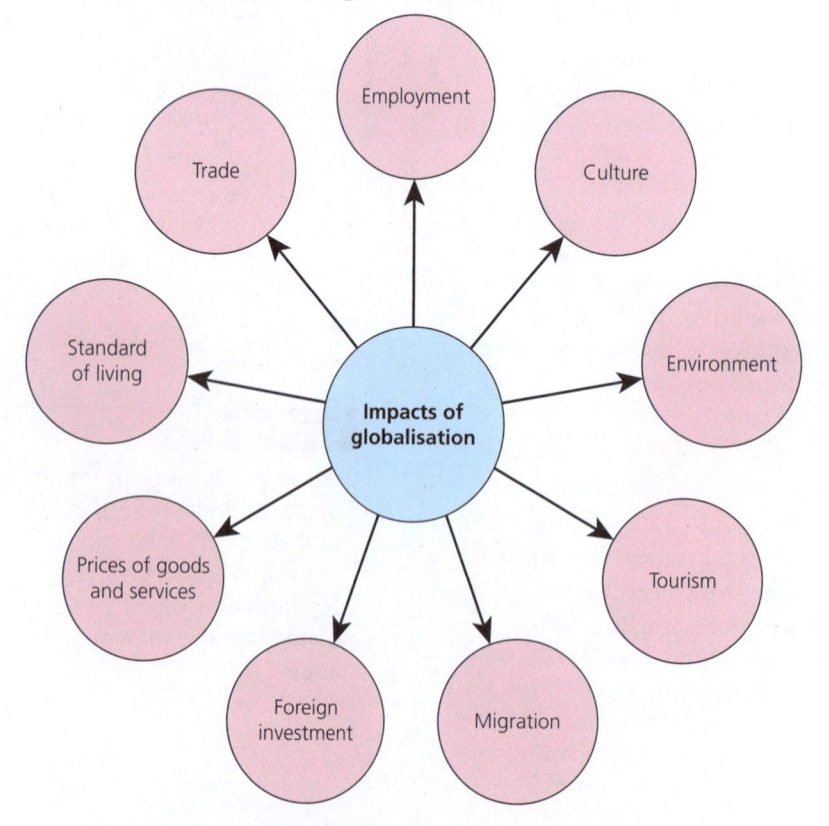

Figure 22.2 Impacts of globalisation

Impact in less developed countries

REVISED

- The term 'less developed countries' covers a wide range of countries and differing levels of development in key areas such as total GDP, population size and natural resources.
- Economic indicators include: lower GDP per capita and lower levels of industrialisation.
- Human indicators include: lower levels of wellbeing, such as shorter life expectancy and limited access to clean water.
- Less developed countries may have a greater risk of poverty and are less resilient when problems affect their economies.

Less developed country
A country with a developing economy that has lower GDP per capita, lower levels of industrialisation and weaker indicators of wellbeing.

Producers

Costs include:

- Vulnerability to problems in the worldwide economy: this is a more significant problem for producers in less developed countries as they already have fewer resources to deal with economic shocks. A reduction in foreign investment or demand for exports can make it difficult for producers to survive.
- Increased migration and loss of skilled workers: many skilled workers may choose to work in a developed country, which leaves a less productive workforce.
- Smaller, developing industries go out of business: these may not be able to compete with bigger businesses worldwide.

Benefits include:

- Wider markets to sell into: there is the potential for increased sales, as producers can now sell worldwide. This may be more difficult for producers in a less developed country who may not have the resources to grow their output and take advantage of potential exports.
- Advances in technology: sharing of scientific information and joint research may lead to reduced costs for producers in less developed countries, but they may take time to filter through.
- Increased foreign investment: this combined with attempts by governments to attract more investment may reduce costs for producers in less developed countries, e.g. more roads may be built, which helps the moving around of people and goods.

Workers

Costs include:

- Increased use of machinery and unemployment: workers may be replaced with machinery to increase productivity, so they can be internationally competitive.
- Increased vulnerability and unemployment: the problem of increasing dependence on world markets is that, if global demand falls for exports from less developed countries, then fewer workers will be needed.
- Increased gap between rich and poor: the increased revenue from more trade may not filter down to workers but may instead be spread between the government, owners and managers.
- Poor working conditions: there may be less regulation in less developed countries, which can create cost advantages for global firms, but leads to poor treatment of workers there such as lower pay and long working hours.

Benefits include:
- Increased employment due to increased output: over time, there should be an increase in employment within a country due to increased output to meet international trade.
- Increased employment due to increased investment: an increase in foreign investment may help less developed countries and provide more jobs for workers.
- Increased geographical mobility: the opening up of markets means that workers from less developed countries have the opportunity to live and work anywhere in the world.

Consumers

Costs include:
- Rising prices: as there are more consumers competing to buy some goods, this can actually lead to an increase in global prices, so consumers in less developed countries, may no longer be able to afford the prices of essential goods, e.g. rice.
- Poor quality of services due to migration: freer movement of people may mean a loss of skilled professionals in less developed countries.

Benefits include:
- Wider range of goods: due to the lowering of barriers to trade and the internet, there should be increased access to a greater range of goods, such as life-saving medicines.
- Access to global brands: the availability of global brands to consumers in less developed countries may be seen as a positive consequence.
- Greater opportunity to travel: the opening up of borders also allows greater tourism for those consumers in less developed countries who can afford to travel.
- Better infrastructure due to foreign investment: consumers may benefit from some of the development linked to foreign investment, e.g. better transport links.

Economic, social and environmental sustainability

Economic sustainability:
- Due to the increase in international trade, there should be greater tax revenues, less unemployment, increased output and economic growth.
- However, the benefits may not last if multinational companies leave e.g. after finding another country with lower costs.
- With bigger, more expert legal and finance departments, there are also examples of tax avoidance by multinational companies, which may mean fewer benefits for the economy.

Social sustainability:
- Increased employment should lead to increased income, which should reduce poverty as workers can afford to buy more goods and services.
- However, these positives should be balanced with the negative effects for society if essential goods rise in price, cultural diversity is lost, and workplace conditions worsen.

Environmental sustainability:
- Globalisation should have a positive impact on environmental sustainability on a worldwide basis because due to increased international trade, countries should now be specialising in the goods they can produce most efficiently, leading to best use of scarce resources.

- However, less developed countries may specialise more in primary and secondary sector markets, with production processes that are more likely to damage the environment.
- Also, less developed countries sometimes rely on natural resources as a key driver of trade and growth. Once these resources are depleted, their economies will face serious problems.

Exam practice

1 Which of the following is NOT likely to be a benefit of globalisation for consumers in the UK?
  A lower prices for goods, e.g. clothes
  B lower quality of services, e.g. NHS
  C better quality of goods, e.g. fruit
  D greater opportunity to travel, e.g. abroad [1]
2 Calculate the percentage change in the world export growth rate between 2013 and 2015. (Give your answer to two decimal places.) [2]

Table 22.1 Growth in world exports 2013–15

	2013	2014	2015
World exports	2.7%	2.7%	3.0%

Source: www.wto.org

3 Explain what is meant by the term 'globalisation'? [2]
4 Explain one cause of globalisation. [2]
5 Explain one factor which might limit less developed countries benefiting from globalisation. [2]
6 Evaluate whether or not the benefits of globalisation are greater than the costs for UK consumers. [6]

Answers and quick quiz 22 online

Summary

You should have an understanding of:
- what globalisation is, including its driving factors
- how development is measured by GDP per capita, life expectancy, access to healthcare, technology, education
- how to evaluate the costs and benefits of globalisation to producers, workers and consumers in developed countries
- how to evaluate the impact of globalisation on economic, social and environmental sustainability in developed countries
- how to evaluate the costs and benefits of globalisation to producers, workers and consumers in less developed countries
- how to evaluate the impact of globalisation on economic, social and environmental sustainability in less developed countries